A Brain-Based Approach
to Closing the Achievement
GAP

A Brain-Based Approach to Closing the Achievement

GAP

Horacio Sanchez

To order additional copies of this book, contact:
Xlibris Corporation
1-888-795-4274
www.Xlibris.com
Orders@Xlibris.com
54394

Contents

INTRODUCTION

The *achievement gap* is a term used to describe the academic deficiencies of all student populations that consistently underperform on standardized testing: minorities, children and adolescents with disabilities, and those living in poverty. Race and poverty appear to be the most obvious common denominators present among underperforming student populations. This observation has led to the supposition that a wide range of risk factors commonly occur among certain minority groups living in poverty and is at the source of the achievement gap. This hypothesis was complicated, however, when testing results revealed that middle-income minority students also consistently underperformed at a rate disproportionate to their nonminority peers. Equally confounding is the fact that a percentage of poor minority students meet and even exceed testing norms. In spite of these inconsistencies in the theory, public education has widely accepted the premise that race and poverty are the primary causes of the achievement gap. However, acceptance of this theory has produced unforeseen consequences. Many teachers perceive that the fight to close the achievement gap is futile since public education cannot be called upon to solve such overwhelming societal problems.

Frustration over public education's inability to close the achievement gap has reached an all-time high. Recent reports revealed that after ten years of focusing on eliminating the problem, the gap is actually widening. Consequently, some teachers now want to focus the fight on repealing the legislation that requires all students to meet uniform academic performance standards prior to graduation rather than on closing the achievement gap. However, public education is currently unable to abandon the cause since legislation such as No Child Left Behind has tied federal funding to the elimination of the problem. In addition, newspapers and television stations have made it a practice to review each state's annual academic performance report. In-depth stories on every school and district that has consistently failed to close the achievement gap have become a common occurrence. The increased publicity has made the achievement gap not only a well-documented problem but also a source of public embarrassment. Currently, educational agencies have begun to tie teacher evaluation, pay increases, bonuses, and even tenure to student performance. However, in many cases these linkages have caused the most qualified teachers to avoid employment at schools with underperforming minority populations, another unintended consequence of efforts to close the gap. The elimination of the achievement gap has become the single most important issue facing public education today.

A Brain-Based Approach to Closing the Achievement Gap reveals that brain science provides a superior framework for understanding the achievement gap. This framework lacks any of the contradictions found in existing theories that focus on race and poverty. Advancements in brain science reveal that chemical imbalance can be caused by anything that triggers anxiety. This is a significant finding because whenever imbalance reaches a certain level, it causes a region in the primitive brain to lower the activity of the cortex, which is intricately involved in learning and the performance of executive functions. In addition, stress hampers the brain's ability to regenerate in the hippocampus, the part of the brain involved in initial learning and short-term memory. This means that persistent stress over time can cause sufficient chemical imbalance to impair any individual's cognitive capacity. Fortunately, however, research also has proven that schools can make simple changes in the school climate to improve the brain's chemical balance. Modifications in instruction also can be made that will allow students suffering from imbalances to be able to compensate and achieve comprehension. Additionally, schools can promote healthier brain function by increasing a specific set of protective factors identified in multiple longitudinal studies. By restoring chemical balance and improving brain function, underperforming students, regardless of race, gender, or financial status, can begin to maximize their academic performance, thus helping to eliminate the achievement gap.

This book attempts to follow some of the scientific guidelines in its formatting. The brain comprehends all-new information based on what it already knows. Therefore to facilitate comprehension, the book attempts to relate new learning to common experiences that a majority of people can relate to. In addition, comprehension of new concepts requires consistent repetition for the learner to gain a working knowledge. As a result, the most significant new concepts are repeated in various chapters in different ways. This avoids the reader's having to refer back constantly to the original explanation. The goal is to facilitate the reader's ability to utilize the information after the initial reading of the book.

CHAPTER 1

The Underpinnings of Human Behavior and the Impact on Education

*The whole problem with the world is that fools and fanatics are always so
certain of themselves, and wiser people so full of doubts.*

– Bertrand Russell

Before I can begin to address the brain and learning, it is important
to step back and put into perspective the larger picture. Learning, broken down to
its simplest equation, is *change*; the brain must make a chemical transformation in
the process of learning and a specific series of structural modifications to produce a
new behavior. Therefore, it is rational to conclude that understanding how the brain
changes is the key to education. It is the key not only to the specific question of how
to improve learning but also to the broader question of how to accomplish systems
change. Systems change is merely collective learning designed to produce long-term
behavioral change. Understanding this concept leads us to realize that effective systems
change must implement advanced learning strategies designed to produce long-term
behavioral change. It is broadly accepted that for any truly significant change to take
place in an educational program, 80 percent of the staff must be in agreement with the
change and willing to commit to some new behavioral practices. Just as it is impossible
to master the complexities of learning without first understanding how the brain
produces behavioral change, it is difficult to achieve true systems change unless we
understand how to influence behavioral change. To understand how humans change,
we must begin with a sound basic understanding of human development through the
four underpinnings of human behaviors.

The first underpinning of human development is genetics: where we start. Genetics
in this case is used to describe the ability of the human brain to produce predictable

change on schedule. Like most mammals, the human brain is born only half-developed. At birth, the brain weighs about 350 grams; at six months, it is at 50 percent of its adult weight; at one year, it is at 60 percent of its adult weight; at two and a half years, it is at 75 percent of its adult weight; at six years, it is at 90 percent of its adult weight; and at ten years, it is at 95 percent of its adult weight. The dance of nature and nurture has been intricately involved from the first moment of development (Rose 2005). Babies born with normal to advanced brain functions will develop according to a genetically preordained pattern that is indicative of the capacity present at birth and the exposure to safe and nurturing environments. When both of these factors are operating as they should, one can predict when certain preordained changes would take place; these changes are called milestones. Understanding this genetic predisposition begins to explain why milestones are so predictive. Milestones are indicative of appropriate regional brain development. They also indicate that certain brain cells are capable of producing their preordained function, as well as possessing the ability to respond appropriately and even adapt to external stimuli. That is why a child with a slight delay in meeting a major milestone is not too disturbing; however, significant delays are representative of substantial cell impairment in the brain.

When significant delay is present, one cannot assume genetic impairment alone. A healthy child still requires safe, predictable environments, appropriate nurturing, and appropriate exposure to required stimuli to meet most milestones. Children born with regional brain impairments are often the same infants who are not receiving predictable nurturing and appropriately stimulating environments. This pattern is predictable because many altered brain functions have hereditary features. Thus, children struggling to meet milestones are often being parented by individuals who might not have the capacity to provide the infant with the structure, nurturing, and consistency he or she needs. Schools can accept this science or continue to blame the victim and be ill prepared to deal with cognitive and behavioral variance.

Ultimately, inferior genetics affects not only the ability of brain cells to produce preprogrammed patterns but also the ability of cells to respond appropriately to external stimuli. These issues are further complicated whenever the environment fails to provide safety, nurturance, and appropriate stimuli. Therefore, students with inferior genetics suffer not only from the inability to do certain functions but also from the ability to adapt well to the ever-changing world. That is why adaptability is the layman's test of mental health. The healthier the brain, the more easily a person is capable of change.

The second underpinning of human behavior is temperament. Temperament is best defined as how a person reacts to stimuli. A stimulus can be anything or, more precisely, everything. Temperament can be understood easily through a simple visual. Imagine the world on a slide rule: on the far left are those individuals with easy temperament, on the far right are those individuals with difficult temperament, and disbursed between the two extreme points are the rest of the world's population.

Those individuals on the far left of the continuum, with easy temperament, are born with the unique ability to establish eating and sleeping patterns easily without much external support; more precisely, they are the children who are born with the cell capacity to adapt quickly. In addition, these individuals do not overact to stimuli, they quickly adjust to change, and they have a remarkable ability to read human nonverbal cues very early in life. Some people refer to this advanced ability to read nonverbal cues as high emotional intelligence. From the beginning of life, these individuals excel in the most important aspect of life, human interaction. They have wonderful affect that seems to draw others to them. Individuals with easy temperament represent only 5 to 10 percent of the population.

On the far right of our continuum are those with difficult temperament. These individuals also represent only 5 to 10 percent of the population. Individuals with difficult temperament struggle to establish healthy eating and sleeping patterns. Not only they are slow to read nonverbal social cues, but also they are prone to misreading these signals in others. This lack of ability will place them at a disadvantage in interpersonal relationships throughout their lives. Because individuals with difficult temperament are slow to adjust to stimuli, they will be more sensitive to any changes in their environment. This sensitivity to stimuli makes them chemically more volatile and, as a result, more at risk for impulsive reactions. This level of constant agitation under which they live will make childcare challenging and frustrating. Also at this end of the spectrum is the shy and anxious temperament. Shy and anxious temperament has all the features of difficult temperament with one main exception. These persons tend to internalize issues. However, a word of caution is warranted here: many aggressors of school violence have shy and anxious temperament. They internalize feelings of being bullied to the point that they begin to fantasize having the power to hurt their attackers. The fantasy world gives way to planning, which leads to action under the right conditions of stress.

Often it is the healthier parents, living well above middle income, whose difficult-temperament or shy – and anxious-temperament children will benefit from childcare support in sufficient amounts to help manage their deficiencies. However, parents who are less prepared might become emotional, frustrated, and even abusive. It is important to note that the child who is most sensitive to stimuli and least capable of understanding his or her environment is the same child who is most at risk for being abused by their childcare providers. If these children are exposed to trauma, the nature of the impulsive behavior becomes more severe. Those with difficult temperament not only have poor response to nonverbal cues but also have very flat affect. This flat affect makes it difficult for others to read and understand them, thus adding to their difficulty in developing relationships. Individuals with difficult temperaments have trouble bonding to others and maintaining relationships. The list of reasons is substantial: they seem always agitated, their nonverbal behaviors appear to be threatening, they constantly misread the intentions of others, and they demonstrate extreme behaviors when they are overly stimulated. The shy and anxious child also is easily agitated but tends to withdraw and to demonstrate nonverbal cues that indicate a high level of anxiety. Healthy children will tend to avoid the shy and anxious child because that child seems different, and at a deeper level, being around him or her will tend to increase their level of anxiety.

It is individuals with difficult or closer to difficult temperaments, coming from unstructured environments, who have the greatest problems adjusting to school. They struggle with the change and with the level of stimulation. Most importantly, since learning is change, the chemical impact of learning can itself cause impulsive and even negative behavior. As a result, there exist portions of the student population that can be negatively impacted by the mere act of being taught something new. That is why teachers must become more adept at introducing the more challenging materials in the context of information that these students already know and are comfortable with. In order to accomplish this, teachers must take the time to find out what students know, spend time doing, and feel that they are good at.

The majority of individuals on the temperament slide rule are in the middle. If these individuals are chemically healthy, they require a short period to adjust to change. And since most individuals are not victims of trauma, they are less likely to exhibit extreme behaviors, even during periods of transition. Because of sheer numbers, schools are often unmotivated to help at-risk students' transition with ease since a significant portion of the school population adjusts in a short period of time. However, to conclude that the learning environment is sufficiently structured and that most students are fine is erroneous. The reality is that in many schools across the nation, students struggle with the social, academic, and even unseen dangers present at most schools. Many students who seem on the surface to be fine suffer from low-grade anxiety. This level of anxiety will not necessarily produce an epidemic of negative behavior, but it does consistently contribute to lower test scores and increased behavioral incidents. There is enough evidence on how the brain functions to allow us to know that even low levels of anxiety reduce cortextual function and increase impulsivity. Therefore, it is logical to establish environments that allow all students to perform at their optimal level. Environments that allow the unhealthiest students to thrive are actually the same environments that allow for optimal achievement by all students.

It is crucial for schools to understand that a significant portion of the student population requires educational environments that are highly ritualized. A ritualized setting is not the same as an environment that has a set of clearly defined rules that are consistently enforced. Ritualized environments do not place the primary emphasis on rules and enforcement. By not focusing on rules and violations, these ritualized settings avoid some of the predictable compulsions to violate rules that are a feature of certain emotional disorders. For example, individuals suffering from either oppositional defiant disorder or conduct disorder cannot help violating rules. These two disorders make up the majority of individuals with behavioral problems. Ritualized environments focus on teaching what the educators want students to do and establishing times when the behavior will be practiced, monitored, and reinforced. Students come to believe that the practice exists for their benefit rather than as a control mechanism. Over time the practice itself becomes familiar and therefore comforting. Highly ritualized settings allow struggling individuals the opportunity to become accustomed to the environment more quickly because it is so predictable.

Once the student becomes accustomed to the rituals that occur throughout the school day, the practices act as an anchor. When participating in the routines, the body and mind grow so accustomed to the occurrence that it actually improves chemical balance. Imagine a student who struggles to adjust, entering school and immediately participating in a very familiar ritual that helps him or her better transition into the school day. Think of the possibilities if the school anchored the educational day with rituals at the beginning, middle, and end of the day. Admission, lunch, and dismissal are highly stimulating unstructured transitions that have always proven problematic for the unhealthy student and even for the healthy student who is experiencing temporary chemical imbalance. It is important to note that the human brain undergoes many periods of dramatic change that create temporary chemical imbalances. According to some neuroscientists, the brain undergoes some fundamental restructuring during adolescence, just as it does during the earliest years of childhood (McCrone 2000). At this time, students need the familiarity of rituals to anchor them while they become accustomed to new stimuli.

At the moment a school begins to see the importance of establishing rituals that improve the educational climate, the concept of systems change begins to take shape. Any valued ritual or practice takes consistent modeling, practice, and even reinforcement. It is the adults in every school setting who must change their behavior in order to achieve educational reform. The initial problem is that school staff reflect a wide range of genetic profiles and temperaments themselves. Staff who are closer to the right – or the difficult temperament – will resist all changes because the transition causes them chemical discomfort. This is not a villainous act but rather a conditioned response pattern that was established early in life. Whenever these individuals experience change, they feel the chemical imbalance in their bodies. The chemical imbalance causes anxiety and produces many of the co-occurring features associated with the condition. Over time, these individuals have learned to protect themselves by resisting change. If a systems change is not supported by a sufficient number of staff, it will not be modeled and reinforced correctly enough to take hold. That is why understanding how behavior change occurs is the cornerstone of effective systems change. Administrators must learn how to institute change in a manner that allows staff right of center to accept and be willing to attempt change.

Establishing the correct rituals will allow students with difficult or shy and anxious temperaments the opportunity for better daily transition to the educational setting. In addition, since learning is change, teaching must place emphasis on shaping new information in the context of what students already know. This requires that teachers find out what information students actually know and are comfortable with. Unfortunately, most teachers assume they know what their students have previously learned. Often this assumption leads to the inability of the difficult-temperament student to learn new material because that student does not have the knowledge base held by others. A lack of understanding of this student profile will lead to frustration, poor academic performance, and eventually negative behaviors.

It is important to reconcile genetics and temperament before going any farther. Reconciliation of these first two underpinnings can help to explain some inconsistencies that puzzle the casual observer of human behavior. For example, why do certain people with outstanding potential become such consistent failures? A person can be born with superior genetics and with a difficult temperament. This combination will reduce this individual's ability to take full advantage of his or her capacity. Although this individual will have an accelerated capacity to learn, the chemical reaction caused by new experiences will slow the learning process until he or she can become familiar enough not to experience anxiety. If this person does not come from a supportive and structured environment, it will take him/her even longer to adjust. This is because the home fails to provide a setting that improves chemical functioning, therefore compounding the individual's problems. This series of events explains how someone with great capacity can struggle to achieve their full potential. Now begin to configure all the possibilities of genetics and temperaments, and you can begin to see clusters of different individual profiles: average genetics and easy temperament, inferior genetics and difficult temperament, superior genetics and shy and anxious temperament, and so on. Education must focus on ways to maximize the productivity of all the configurations in every school. A universal starting point is creating highly routine and nurturing environments. These structured educational settings assist all the different genetic and temperament configurations in excelling. Educational settings that do not teach routines to help individuals better transition have already swung the pendulum toward those students in the center and to the left of our temperament slide rule and away from those students who need help the most.

I have always said, tongue in cheek, that it is healthy students who have ruined the educational system. As long as educators can point to those students achieving and being successful in less structured settings, there will not be enough motivation to invest the time and energy needed to create optimum educational settings for all students. This simple conclusion might provide profound insight into the age-old question of who is education designed for. Although Western education mandates the participation of everyone under the age of sixteen, the system is clearly designed for people with average to superior genetics possessing normal to easy temperament.

The third underpinning of human behavior is exposure: what we already have adjusted to. Adjustment to new stimuli requires a sufficient level of exposure to reduce significant levels of chemical reaction. Those who navigate life more adeptly have had a greater level of exposure, increasing their ability to adapt to new experiences. Individuals who have a breadth of exposure can draw from a wide range of experiences to help understand new situations without becoming overly stimulated. Individuals with difficult temperament will adjust better to everyday life if they have been carefully exposed to experiences that will help them navigate common situations. That kind of exposure before entering school will make many of the activities required in early education familiar or at least more understandable. However, consider the student who has average genetics, is closer to difficult temperament, and is born into poverty. One of the consistent products of poverty is the lack of life exposure. It is now commonly known that individuals in poverty can spend a lifetime within a five- to ten-mile radius of their homes. Recent studies have shown that 66 percent of trips taken by individuals living in poverty are three miles or less (Murakami and Young 1997). Such limited exposure predisposes these individuals to become overly stimulated by the most mundane of new situations, thus producing chemical imbalance. In addition, what one has been exposed to is predictive of what the brain will focus on. Imagine a child with average genetics and difficult temperament who has had limited exposure entering a large and highly stimulating environment. The child's brain in this new social setting will seek understanding by first looking for what he or she already knows. If nothing that can provide understanding is found, then anxiety will rise. It is anxiety mixed with past trauma that is a volatile formula for schools.

Let us now put together genetics, temperament, and exposure to help understand clusters of individual profiles. For example, take a person with superior genetics, closer to difficult temperament, and limited life exposure. Although this individual possesses outstanding genetic capacity, he or she will struggle in two ways. First, because of temperament, he or she will take longer to adjust to new stimuli. Then, because of his or her lack of exposure, more stimuli will be new, less of it will be appropriately comprehended, and more of it will be viewed as threatening, causing overarousal. The sad fact is that many students with this very profile are even more at risk for school failure because they often come from unstructured homes that do not model or teach skills that teachers expect students to already possess. Schools can begin to better manage these students' transition into school by having preschool programs focus on the daily practice of skills and behaviors needed to better manage transition into school. It is not enough to teach and practice these skills briefly; they have to become ritualized practices that become so familiar that they do not produce chemical arousal but, instead, improve chemical disposition. Skills like group cooperation need to be taught to students who lack exposure and suffer from increased anxiety in social settings.

The fourth underpinning of human behavior concerns highly emotional experiences: how you react when chemically aroused. The human brain stores highly emotional experiences differently from other information learned or experienced. The amygdala is the part of the brain most involved in highly emotional behavior. It stores highly emotional experiences, configures the chemical responses, and remembers those chemical responses forever. By remembering each previous response, it can reproduce that response even faster in the future. Most importantly, when significantly aroused, the amygdala secretes chemicals that reduce interference from the cortex. The cortex is in charge of storing what has been learned long-term and for producing reasonable and rational behavior. When an individual is overly aroused, he or she will be prone to produce behaviors that are based on past emotional experiences. This begins to explain why individuals exposed to abuse or neglect are more prone to negative behaviors that produce detrimental consequences.

In addition, many of the students who are subjected to repetitive trauma are prone to misperceiving benign situations as threatening whenever they become too aroused. It·is this unpredictable volatility that places this profile student at greater risk for behaviors that result in school separation and failure. That is because most school administrators cannot comprehend why the student demonstrated such extreme behaviors in response to a given situation. However, this student is responding to the situation that just happened based on his/her responses to past traumas. Therefore, the most important intervention for this student is to create an environment that lowers chemical arousal and helps the student feel safe. Sadly, most schools continue to manage this profile student by resolving each incident through countless hours of meeting, planning, interventions, and measures that fail to reduce the primary triggers in the school environment that produce higher levels of arousal. The result will be many unsuccessful attempts to resolve each individual incident rather than understanding the cause of the behavior, followed by the determination that the student requires more supervision than the educational setting is capable of providing.

In reconciling all four underpinnings of human behavior, we can begin to understand the full range of human behavior and the variables that are always involved. For example, a person with superior genetics, difficult temperament, and poor exposure will struggle to adjust in spite of genetic capacity. If the child has been exposed to abuse and neglect, he or she will constantly be prone to extreme behaviors. On the other hand, an individual with average to inferior genetics with easy temperament and wide ranges of life exposure will be more prone to maximizing potential. If that person has not been exposed to abuse and neglect, he or she will cope with highly stimulating situations better and, when overwhelmed, will be less likely to resort to extreme negative actions.

With the above mentioned information, it is now easy to understand the convergence of circumstances that produce the most-difficult-to-educate students. Imagine an individual born with inferior genetics. The inability to produce preordained patterns, respond appropriately to external stimuli, and deal constantly with chemical imbalance radically reduces his or her ability to cope with life. Let's say that this individual is also born with difficult temperament, making everything experienced and learned result in increased chemical imbalance. Over time, individuals with this profile will begin to avoid new experiences and information because they are keenly aware of how anxious newness makes them feel. In addition, the inability to maintain good sleeping and eating patterns only further compounds their chemical imbalance. These children are not helped but are indeed hurt by an unstructured, abusive environment that hinders their chemical improvement, thus producing extreme behaviors when they are chemically aroused. In addition, the chemical imbalance leads to the students' easy arousal in new situations, even if they are benign. Finally, these children will have limited life exposure, making every new experience only more difficult because they have little past information to draw upon to navigate change.

If education better prepares to manage the troubled student profiles described above, then it will have established the exact educational climate and culture that will help maximize every student's academic achievement and behavioral development. This new climate and culture will lead to improved test scores and lower behavioral incidents across the entire student body spectrum.

CHAPTER 2

Curriculum

The highest result of education is tolerance.

– Helen Keller

The definition of the term *curriculum* in Western culture was highly influenced by the historical circumstances and prevalent beliefs of the time period from which it emerged. Many believe that the first published attempt to define the term *curriculum* was in 1918 by John Franklin Bobbitt. He believed that *curriculum* was a course of deeds and experiences that would allow every child to become a contributing member of society. Bobbitt thought that scientific experts possessed the background and knowledge to identify what qualities were desirable in a member of society and what experiences would produce these desired qualities.

It is not surprising that Bobbitt's notion of curriculum was quickly rejected. The argument given was that his definition ignored the fact that people cannot all have carefully designed experiences. Bobbitt's interpretation of curriculum was labeled social engineering. Social engineering as defined by Bobbitt's critics was the programming of human beings to fulfill predetermined roles in the social order.

It is unlikely that Bobbitt's notion of curriculum was rejected solely on the merits of his ideas. This is a safe conclusion because the human brain understands everything presented based on what it already knows. Therefore, new ideas are often rejected due to a lack of preexisting related information to aid in its comprehension. More importantly, the human brain filters information emotionally. The amygdala, the emotional center of the brain, monitors all stimuli processed by the brain to determine if it poses a threat. The amygdala provides this filter because its primary role is survival. Since the amygdala also activates emotional memories, anything that challenges existing values often triggers an emotional response. The problem with emotional response is that if the level of arousal is high enough, it will prohibit interference from the cortex, the part of the brain in charge of logic and reasoning. Therefore, throughout history, many new ideas have been met with emotionally driven actions often carried out under the guise of protecting man. Many proponents of new thoughts have been tortured and killed. These emotional reactions cannot be seen as a rational response to new ideas.

A brief review of the historical setting at the time of Bobbitt's theory on curriculum reveals southern whites denying blacks their civil rights based on the argument that they were less than human and inferior to whites. Native Americans were being forced onto small reservations and separated from American society because they were deemed savages. Thirty-seven million immigrants were being used as a source of cheap labor for the industrial movement; this behavior was justified because these people were different in language, dress, and culture. In this setting, a notion that everyone can achieve great value to his or her society flew in the face of the beliefs held by many in power. They believed in a natural order, that some individuals' roles in life were to perform the menial tasks so that those more advanced could tend to more important issues. Thus, it is only logical that the definition of curriculum would be influenced by the issues concerning human equality taking place at the time.

Around the same time, John Dewey (October 1859–June 1952) had become a leader in the pragmatist movement and an advocate for educational reform. The pragmatists believed that each individual's life is provided meaning based on the individual's contributions to society. In addition, the pragmatists believed that affording everyone access to education should be society's vehicle for providing this opportunity.

Those who opposed educational reform utilized an obscure passage penned by Dewey as justification for the utilization of education as a vehicle for determining who is most suitable to lead and take a more prominent role in society:

> Consider for example the activities of bees in contrast with the changes in the sands when the wind blows them about. The results of the bees' actions may be called ends not because they are designed or consciously intended, but because they are true terminations or completions of what has preceded. When the bees gather pollen and make wax and build cells, each step prepares the way for the next. When cells are built, the queen lays eggs in them; when eggs are laid, they are sealed and bees brood them and keep them at a temperature required to hatch them. When they are hatched, bees feed the young until they can take care of themselves. (John Dewey, *Democracy and Education*, 1916)

Those in power soon claimed that educational reform and industrialization were aligned. The position they stated was that education would help determine who the drones would be and what tasks for the good of society they would fulfill. The interesting thing is that they selected a paragraph that was in a book that strongly contradicted their conclusions.

Those in power knew that they could not turn back the clock on educational reform. Thus they decided to reframe Dewey's own words. They utilized this passage to mean that education should become the tool to determine everyone's role in society. It is clear that Dewey did not intend this passage to be used in this manner because he saw education as providing an opportunity for everyone to reach his/her capacity. It is during this period that curriculum begins to emerge as a method for evaluating individual capacity. Although education becomes a right and not a privilege, it also becomes the vehicle for determining who is appropriate for the careers most valued by society. It is here that the definition of curriculum begins to mean courses of study and their contents, as well as the methods of evaluation. Simply put, curriculum started to have less to do with how children learn and more to do with what they learn and how they are tested.

The reason that this is a true departure from what Dewey intended is illustrated in the way he ran his schools. Dewey believed that the study of human behavior provided a framework for how education should be delivered. He said that experience has shown that when children have a chance to engage in physical activities while learning, learning becomes tied into their natural impulse to play. When education is delivered in this manner, children enjoy school, are easier to manage, and learn more efficiently. He conjectured that if teachers stopped using play, games, and constructive occupations only as a relief from the tedium and strain of "regular" schoolwork, education would be better delivered. Therefore, Dewey concluded that curriculum should incorporate these interactive components into regular school programs. Unfortunately, Dewey's schools did not become the model for education; later they closed. His message on the importance of how children learn was lost in a social period when importance had shifted to the fulfillment of societal roles.

The transition from how people learn to what they should learn and how they should be evaluated might be at the core of the achievement gap. The sad thing is that if Dewey's instructional philosophies had been carried out, he might have been known as the father of brain-based instruction. At the core of brain-based instruction is sensory-integrated teaching that makes learning an experience. Dewey observed that children of all backgrounds were given the opportunity to achieve when provided instruction that aligned with how the brain naturally learns.

CHAPTER 3

Teaching Format

In teaching it is the method and not the content that is the message.
– Ashley Montague

A Brain-Based Approach to Education

Much has been made of what students are taught in American schools; we have national standards and detailed curricula and courses of study to guide us through every grade level. We have a multitude of tests to assess what has been learned by whom. Ironically, with all this attention on learning, little has been written concerning how the required knowledge will be imparted and what correlations might exist between educational approaches and effective outcomes. We also witness that every year, more and more students are diagnosed with learning disabilities and other pathologies that impede their ability to learn. The reality is that most of these impediments are a direct result of altered brain function resulting from biological and/or environmental factors. This altered brain function has a direct correlation to the way one perceives one's environment, how easily one is able to adapt, and how well one is able to learn and retain the lessons taught in school.

The brain functions at an optimal level when chemical secretions in the brain are well regulated and maintained within normal limits. Once outside of this "normal" range, the brain is less able to learn. Information in the brain is processed through cells called neurons. They are the only cells that process information. Emotion signals the neurons to send messages chemically. Neurotransmitters send little sacks of chemicals and spew the contents to neuroreceptors (also called dendrites) that receive the information. One neuron can communicate with as many as twenty thousand others. The brain has one hundred billion neurons, and they all have the capacity to communicate with twenty thousand other neurons. This is what makes the brain such a complex organ. A healthy brain knows when to send chemical messages, how much chemicals to send, and how to process each chemical in order to produce an action. Basically, this chemical process accounts for every thought, action, and word we produce. This explains why pathology and cognitive deficits can be summed up as altered brain chemistry. Damage to neurotransmitters or neuroreceptors will produce abnormal chemical levels in the brain. When these abnormal levels are processed, they result in abnormal behavior. Neurotransmitter and neuroreceptor damage can be the result of a hereditary condition of one's parents, stress experienced by the mother during gestation, traumatic experiences, or long-term depravity, to pinpoint just a few of the most prevalent causes.

When chemical secretions are not appropriately regulated, the body's entire system is altered: heart, blood vessels, lungs, skin, sweat, salivary glands, muscles, digestion, and the immune system (Ferris 1996). Individuals who suffer from pathology have brain chemistry secretion patterns that are outside the brain's optimal range of functioning. For example, children who exhibit aggression have altered secretions of the chemical serotonin found in the brain. Abnormal secretions of other chemicals will impact other behaviors.

Altered secretion patterns impact not only the back region of the brain that is in charge of survival, but also the midbrain that controls eating and sleeping patterns. That is why those who are experiencing the stress of a divorce, deadlines at work, or the death of a loved one often experience temporary chemical changes in the brain resulting in disturbed eating and/or sleeping patterns. This also explains why so many psychiatric diagnoses identify altered eating and sleeping patterns as an indicator of an existing pathology. Remember, pathology and cognitive deficits can be defined as altered brain chemistry. The impact of altered brain chemistry on the hippocampus and the midbrain will have a ripple effect on the brain's entire system. The limbic system is known as the seat of human emotions. It tells us when to run or fight. In simple terms, it determines how the body reacts to charged stimuli, real or perceived. Before the limbic system reacts to the stimulus, however, it consults the cortex, that part of the brain that is in charge of reasoning and executive functions. The cortex takes in data and searches for related information in order to help us reach a reasonable decision in the face of life's stressors. It then communicates with the limbic system in order to justify or to reduce the level of emotional response. However, if chemical secretions overwhelm the limbic system, it will override the cortex and make decisions that can only be categorized as impulsive.

It is this level of impulsivity and misperception that causes many children suffering from psychological and emotional problems to behave in a manner that appears irrational. It is important to remember that behavioral problems are a direct result of genetic or experiential factors that alter the brain's ability to handle the body's chemical secretion patterns. It is known that at the right frontal insula, the state of your body, state of your brain, and external stimuli all intersect (Blakeslee and Blakeslee 2007, pp. 44–51). The condition of any of these three factors can alter perception. Emotions, physical pain, and overstimulation consistently alter what people perceive. It is clear that chemical secretion patterns alter one's ability to process.

The inability of the brain to handle the body's chemical secretions can result in individuals whose brains constantly operate outside the range required for learning and adaptability. Children who suffer from an inability of their brains to manage their bodies' chemical patterns are often the same individuals who experience mounting risk factors. The increased level of risk results in more dramatic shifts in body chemistry, producing the dramatic shifts in brain chemicals that are correlated with emotional and psychiatric illness.

What is known about how the brain functions should be incorporated into every teaching process and practice in order to help high-risk children and their families understand what is happening and learn ways to deal with the problems when they arise. Clinical practices should attempt to deliver information and services in a manner that improves the brain's level of functioning and never diminishes it. It is only then that much of what is being taught can be learned, processed, remembered, and translated into positive action. This is the secret to achieving long-term behavioral change and enhancing cognitive performance.

Therefore, it is only rational that the process for presenting any curriculum must provide an educational paradigm that effectively utilizes what is known about how individuals learn. The brain learns, processes, and adapts information best when it is at its optimal level of functioning. There are some simple strategies that can improve the brain's ability to receive new information.

Utilizing Brain-Based Strategies

The universal definition for physical, emotional, and cognitive disability is the inability of one or more chemicals to be processed appropriately in the brain. Remember, a simplified explanation of brain process is that neurotransmitters send discrete chemicals to neuroreceptors through dendrites to be processed. The configuration and location of brain chemical dispersion account for every function of a human being. Prior to any action, there must be a chemical movement in the brain. Thus, failure to perform a physical function or cognitive task or to manage emotional processes is a result of a chemical imbalance in the brain. Most medications seek to correct chemical imbalance. It is difficult, however, to replicate the precise chemical transfer that the brain produces. As a result, medication is an imperfect attempt to impact the most complicated and advanced machinery on earth: the human brain.

- Resiliency Education Program (REP) is a training model that mimics the brain's process not only for learning but also for establishing new values required to establish and maintain new practices. The approach has determined that true systemic change cannot occur unless 80 percent of staff value the same goal and maintain the established practices for successful implementation. REP advocates that brain-based approaches must be utilized on every level of an educational agency to maximize efficiency, thus impacting how administrators, teachers, parents, and mentors communicate and teach one another as well as the students.
- REP incorporates the following brain-based strategies:
  - Repetition
  - Chunking
  - Music
  - Symbols
  - Movement
  - Senses

During the past decade, advancements in brain research have provided insight as to how the brain learns, how value systems are established, and what determines persistent behaviors. REP not only designed its training and supervision based on these principles but also trains school staff to apply the same principles toward their students.

The brain learns most readily when the teaching process incorporates repetition, chunks of information, music, symbolic association, movement, and the senses. The brain determines value by the simple process of repetition. The brain learns new information by a sequence of chemical transference by neurotransmitters to neuroreceptors through dendrites. Dendrites form a connection between neurons to enable the flow of chemicals. When new information is first learned, the chemical transference through the dendrite is slow and inefficient. Each time the process is repeated, however, the chemical transfer becomes faster and more efficient. When new information is truly learned, the dendrites involved become more robust. It is this repetitive process that helps the brain distinguish important information that should be easily accessible. Therefore, repetition is a proven educational strategy that should be consistently incorporated. Teachers working to help their students experience academic success in schools must make sure that repetition is a consistently utilized method. In today's climate of standardized curricula and mandated testing, however, teachers feel compelled to cover all the material that might be on the statewide end-of-year test. The speed at which the material is covered and the lack of emphasis on any particular information through review place students suffering from chemical imbalances or from environments in which it is difficult to be disciplined in study at risk for continued failure. As a result, only students with good study habits who review on their own and students who have had previous exposure to the material will thrive under these circumstances.

The brain also prefers to receive new information in chunks, which is the reduction or breakdown of information into groupings of three, four, or five. A sequence of numbers is more easily retained by simply breaking it into chunks. A good example of this concept is a phone number: 9193084298 versus 919-308-4298. The key is to take central concepts that a student will need to succeed and reduce them to chunks that are called catch phrases. This process enhances the learning and retention of the student. And can be utilized to assist students in learning new academic and behavioral concepts. Catch phrases also allow new information that is initially not accepted to become more readily acceptable. If a viewpoint is presented in a consistent manner, such as a catchy phrase, over a period of time it will grow in acceptance. Kimberlee Weaver, a psychologist at Virginia Polytechnic University, recently completed a study that showed that a viewpoint heard multiple times from one person or multiple times from several people begins to grow in both popularity and acceptance (Wenner 2007, p. 13). Brain research indicates that a concept reduced to a repeated catch phrase will begin to lose irritation when the idea becomes familiar; ultimately, the brain will begin to think that it always held the viewpoint. Students with poor temperaments and from limited background often require repetition when learning new information that does not correlate with what they already know. The repetition approach allows the teacher to have a method of review that is effective and efficient.

In addition, chunks tend to attach themselves to brain clusters, collections of related information stored in the brain. As a result, they can act as keys in unlocking related information that has been learned. When a person has a wealth of knowledge on a topic, he or she possesses a cluster of neurons dedicated to storing, processing, and retrieving that information. Therefore, relating chunks to existing brain clusters improves the likelihood that the information will progress to long-term memory.

Music should be incorporated by teachers in instruction, both as a strategy for learning and in setting a climate when working with students. Music advances learning. A region of the brain has neurons that can be stimulated only by music. The stimulation of these neurons enhances the learning process by increasing focus, language acquisition, memorization, and abstract reasoning. A multitude of studies have demonstrated that music exposure, participation, and learning consistently increase verbal and math scores. Simply adding a rhythmic pattern to the review process will enhance student recall and storage. Many students who struggle with language comprehension can be aided in learning information through singing it. This approach allows dedicated neurons to be active in the learning process by using stimuli that they are programmed to be responsive to.

Music also impacts the body's heart and blood rate. As a result, music can be a valuable tool in behavior management. The use of music to set a tone or to shift moods is a technique that enhances the teacher's effectiveness. Teachers should seek to utilize music to ease major transitions and as a behavioral intervention. The National Institute of Music (NIM) determined that certain tones have positive effects on the brain. Exposing students consistently to certain identified tones can reduce their levels of stress, physical pain, and anger. The most remarkable finding by the NIM in this study is that just a two-week intervention utilizing tones can have long-term benefits on actual brain structure.

Recent studies in language development have indicated that children and adolescents who demonstrate behavioral problems and difficulty learning consistently lag in the area of language development. It is now known that damage to the hippocampus often occurs in children who experience depravity, abuse, early disease, or who are at hereditary risk for altered hippocampal functioning. Damage to the hippocampus slows learning. Many individuals with a damaged hippocampus have difficulty learning new concepts unless the concept is associated with a symbolic identifier. Everyone learns concepts more quickly when the ideas are associated with symbolic triggers. This approach is consistently utilized in advertisement through logos and other symbols that trigger the recall of information attached to the symbol. The same technique is crucial in teaching new concepts to students at risk of academic failure. Teachers working with at-risk populations must become versed in having concepts reduced to catch phrases and associating them with symbols. This kind of grouping of brain-based strategies has been found to improve academic performance significantly. By grouping these strategies, teachers can appeal to many regions of the brain simultaneously and improve the odds of compensating for any regional deficits a student might have. It is important that educators be trained in this approach in order for them to internalize the practice and effectively use symbols when working with students.

The utilization of movement in the learning process allows for thousands of motor neurons in the basal ganglia, thalamus, and cerebellum that link the brain and the muscles to form a group of tightly dedicated neurons that will produce a consistent chemical message to a given movement stimulus. As a result, ritualized movements coupled with information make up an effective method of improving recall even in students with cognitive deficits. Movement not only helps recall, but also enhances focus, language acquisition, and problem-solving skills. Additionally, it has been shown to repair damaged regions of the brain. Teachers and aides working with at-risk populations should be trained to utilize movement in learning and in promoting healthy, active lifestyles.

All the other senses work on the same principles as movement. Each sense is processed in multiple regions of the brain as well as in the cortex. Whenever information is consistently aligned with the senses, it forms a link between the neurons dedicated to the sense and the cortex. This linkage is called long-term potentiation (LTP). LTP allows for storage in different locations in the brain and increased opportunity for retrieval. The utilization of these practices in learning and behavior management is not only sound practice but also crucial to the success of all children with cognitive or emotional issues.

The premise of utilizing brain-based strategies is simple. When any new information is learned utilizing a brain-based strategy, it increases the likelihood that it will enter short-term memory, that it will be stored in multiple regions of the brain, and that ultimately, it will enter long-term memory and be easily retrieved. Teachers working with at-risk populations should not only learn brain-based strategies but also seek to utilize a minimum of three strategies each time they address crucial subject matter. For example, many of the reading programs that are rooted in brain science train teachers to utilize all the above mentioned techniques on a daily basis. Many of these programs review phonemic skills daily. The review incorporates rhythm and a body movement. The teacher is trained to increase the speed at which students apply what has been learned. Speed is a clear indicator that learning has been fortified and coded appropriately for quick access in the future. The rule of grouping brain-based strategies should be adhered to if the goal is to teach all children because cognitive and psychological disorders are a result of altered brain functions.
Students suffering from academic, emotional, and behavioral problems all have regions of their brains that do not function at an optimal level.

The ability to process language accurately requires a range of chemical balance that is considered average to optimal because the brain must act in concert since there is not a specific language center in the brain. Processing spoken language, reading, and writing are skills that require multiple regions in the brain to function in concert to produce the appropriate outcome. If teachers working with at-risk populations utilize a range of brain-based strategies, information will be processed and stored in multiple regions of the brain. This approach allows the brain to compensate for an impaired region that may interfere with the ability to retain lessons that are primarily taught through language.

Many of the behavioral incidents that occur at schools are directly related to students not being able to process new information, causing mounting frustration and stress. The buildup of anxiety coupled with the perception that the student cannot learn is the root cause of many behaviors that have thrown schools into crisis situations.

CHAPTER 4

Crisis

Crises refine life. In them you discover what you are.
– Allan K. Chalmers

C*risis* is best defined as an outcome resulting from a dramatic shift in chemicals produced by the brain that alerts the amygdala of a threat or a perceived threat. The failure to understand this scientific process has led to many misperceptions and much ill-advised planning related to crisis.

The one thing schools cannot be completely prepared for is handling crisis. That is because the very nature of a crisis is that the unexpected has occurred. In these emotional situations, it is impossible to predict with certainty how anyone will react. In addition, once a crisis has occurred, the long-term damage usually has already taken place. Emotional situations are stored differently in the brain, and past behavioral responses can be triggered again even more quickly by any new event that triggers a high-enough level of arousal. This means that once a student demonstrates a negative response when aroused, he or she is more likely to repeat the behavior the next time stress or anxiety rises. Teachers who struggle emotionally at the time of the crisis will have those feelings resurface during the next crisis as well. If the emotions the teacher is feeling are closely associated with a student, then the mere presence of the student can trigger feelings of anxiety in the teacher. This is why teachers often seek the removal of students after a crisis; they do not like the constant feeling of anxiety that they experience when in the students' presence. Science indicates that 75 percent of all negative behaviors can be managed only through prevention. Schools need to focus on prevention rather than spending the majority of time planning how best to respond. Focusing on how to respond to crisis will not lower the occurrence of crisis. Neurobiological studies indicate that once the crisis occurs, there are actually very few interventions that can restore chemical balance quickly. Therefore, there really is no such thing as crisis management. We can only react to crisis.

Crisis is a chemical reaction in the brain. When the chemicals that trigger the amygdala have surged to a point that a crisis response has occurred, the chemical levels in the brain and body will require sufficient time to return to normal levels. A consistent misperception related to crisis management is that the proper intervention can restore order immediately. Brain science proves otherwise. The chemical process in the brain requires a sufficient amount of time to return to normative levels. How quickly stabilization occurs is dependent on a wide range of variables.

There are two significant variables that determine how fast someone can recover from crisis. One variable is dependent on the individual's overall health. Individuals who have no preexisting chemical imbalances naturally respond better to crisis; it takes more time to trigger a crisis response, and it takes less time to restore homeostasis, or chemical balance. As noted earlier, all emotional disorders are results of chemical imbalances in one or more brain regions. That is why medications that treat emotional disorders target chemicals in the brain that need to be enhanced or reduced in order to restore homeostasis.

The second variable is the nature of the crisis itself. Crisis usually falls into two main categories: a significant event or a sequence of stressful events. One should not be interpreted as less severe than the other. The issue of severity is ultimately determined by the level of chemical imbalance produced by the event or mounting stressors.

Usually a chemical surge in the brain that produces a crisis response can last from twenty minutes to two hours, depending on the preexisting condition of the person and the severity of the event. However, for individuals who are at risk for succumbing to chemical reactions that meet the definition of crisis, the chemical effects of crisis can linger for up to two days. This is most likely where the term on edge originated: it describes individuals who tend to overreact to nonthreatening stimuli because their chemical condition has never fully stabilized.

Not only does crisis impact a wide range of brain functions; crisis impacts the body as well. A dramatic chemical surge or a consistent chemical imbalance will change heart and blood rate. That is why persons who experience any event that startles them, such as a car accident, find that their heart and blood rate speed up until the chemical that spiked lowers. The work of Porter, Porges, and Marshall looked at how the tone between the heartbeats (the vagal tone) is dramatically altered by stress (Porter et al. 1988, pp. 495–505). Their findings concluded that during crisis, even the resting rhythm of an individual's heartbeat is negatively impacted. Therefore, the impact of long-term stress can cause negative physical complications in body function. Porter, Porges, and Marshall also looked at infants whose vagal tones were higher than those of the normal population due to temperament and were able to predict the occurrence of emotional and physical complications (Porter et al. 1988, pp. 495–505).

The midbrain is in charge of appetite and sleeping. This region of the brain is extremely sensitive to any abnormal chemical levels in the brain. That is why the functions of eating and sleeping are quickly impacted by stress and why focusing on a stressful event prior to falling asleep is liable to have a negative impact on an individual's ability to fall asleep, sleep through the night, or experience restful sleep. Impaired sleeping poses an additional problem for learning. It is during sleep that the brain fortifies new knowledge and makes associations between things learned. The ability to make associations between information represents some of the highest forms of learning: applied knowledge, independent thinking, and creative thought. Individuals experiencing poor sleeping patterns often experience reduced ability to recall. This is because the brain, without adequate sleep, has been unable to fortify what has been learned or to make repairs to brain circuitry.

Although the brain makes up only 2 percent of the human body, it uses 20 percent of the body's metabolic fuel. The brain requires stabilized blood glucose to operate at an optimal level. Glucose levels are best maintained through complex carbohydrates rather than simple sugars, such as whole-grain breads, legumes, and vegetables. In England, A. Wesnes of Northumbria University performed a study on sixty-four students between the ages of six and eleven. He showed that as glucose levels fell, so did students' mental acuity and memory (as discussed in Kiefer 2007, pp. 58–61). Breakfast and healthy snacking throughout the day is required for an optimally functioning brain.

The important role sleeping and eating play in brain function explains why altered eating and sleeping patterns are reliable indicators of emotional disorders. It is important to remember that the definition of an emotional disorder is altered chemical functions in the brain. The mere act of altering chemical levels impacts sleeping and eating. Once they have been impacted long enough, they will impact every other human function. The work of Michael Macht has proven that diet affects not only health and emotion but also the ability to think (2007, pp. 64–69).

The traditional area of the brain most associated with the occurrence of crisis is the limbic system, which is in charge of crisis response. This system is primarily made up of the hippocampus and the amygdala. The limbic system is highly integrated with the entire brain and body. The hippocampus is the librarian of the brain. Every sensory input that is encountered is processed through the hippocampus and sent to appropriate regions of the brain for further storage and processing. The hippocampus plays an important role in memory. Explicit memory, also called emotional memory because it triggers physiological response, is a function of the hippocampus. During any emotional event, the hippocampus is recording every sensory input: smell, taste, touch, sight, and hearing.

The hippocampus has a constant exchange of information with the amygdala. The primary role of the amygdala is survival. All sensory input must pass through the amygdala to determine the level of threat. If the amygdala is aroused, the sensory input becomes explicit, and the hippocampus will not only input data and pass it on to additional regions of the brain for recording and further analysis, but will also retain every nuance of the event as part of the survival system. When the survival system is alerted, the cortex quickly retrieves additional data in order to help the amygdala make a rational response to the perceived threat. The cortex provides the amygdala with any related files held in long-term memory related to the experience. The cortex will continue to retrieve a wide range of related data until the amygdala response is either aborted or disconnected.

Since the amygdala is in charge of survival, it is designed for instantaneous action. It is logical that in times of immediate danger, overprocessing could increase one's level of risk. It is the evolution of the cortex that has allowed man access to a vast array of information not held in the limbic system in order to promote more rational responses. However, in order to ensure safety, when the level of arousal reaches a point at which the amygdala perceives an immediate threat, it will then cut off all information from the cortex and rely solely on data input from the limbic system. This happens because the limbic system has the most sophisticated data file on every sensory input related to past threats. The amygdala's role, then, is to determine the appropriate response and signal for the release of chemicals in the brain through the bloodstream, which will produce immediate action.

Certain problems can occur related to this survival system. A consistent pattern of threat can produce a hypersensitive limbic system. For example, if John was sexually abused one night by his drunken father, the hippocampus would record all the possible sensory data related to the event. It would record the sounds heard when Dad returned home, staggered up the hallway, and slammed open John's bedroom door. The hippocampus would record the light contrast caused by the light in the hallway entering a dark room. It would record the pungent odor of alcohol. The hippocampus would record every aspect of the sexual attack through every sense that was triggered. The amygdala, at the point of determining that Dad was a threat, would release the signal for the appropriate response: first, to try to escape and, next, to fight. If the abuse continues, the amygdala, when aroused, will seek to get sensory input from the hippocampus concerning the abuse, and no additional information will be provided by the cortex that would slow the speed of determining the appropriate response.

The amygdala not only releases the chemical for crisis response but also remembers the exact configuration to enable a quicker release of the same chemical configuration in the face of a similar threat in the future. After a pattern of consistent abuse, John's amygdala will seek to increase the opportunities for survival by releasing the chemical configuration more quickly, such as releasing the signal to react to the sexual attack before his father begins attacking him. In the face of persistent sexual abuse, John's amygdala will continue to search for quicker release of the configured chemical response: early on when he opens the bedroom door, later when he hears him stagger down the hallway, and ultimately even when Dad leaves the home in the evening. This hypersensitive limbic system is sensory driven. Any stimuli associated with the event can trigger the crisis response.

The amygdala is even capable of further reducing outside input during a crisis response. It does not require sensory data from the hippocampus in extreme situations. In all cases of extreme emotion, the amygdala records what is referred to as subconscious memory. For example, Joseph LeDoux discovered that after a trauma in which a sense was highly activated, the loss of that sense would not prevent the amygdala from still subconsciously reacting (1996, pp. 179–224). LeDoux induced phobias in rats that were triggered by sound, and then rendered the rats' auditory cortex inoperable (making the rat consciously deaf). Although the rat could not hear the trigger, the amygdala still was able to sense and react to the stimulus. These findings begin to explain why individuals with hypersensitive limbic systems can be triggered by stimuli they cannot consciously identify.

The subconscious response of the amygdala also begins to explain the importance of perception and brain chemistry. What is perceived by the brain determines chemical response. The cortex attempts to receive accurate sensory input and quickly looks for similar files in the brain to determine what the stimulus is. If the hippocampus has explicit memories triggered by the stimulus, it will begin to change the interpretation based on past strong emotional memories. If the stimulus was threatening, the amygdala's subconscious memory system can override the sensory assessments of the cortex and hippocampus, producing a new reality. As a result, emotional perception is the strongest reality. It dictates chemical response in the brain.

Many crisis situations that are difficult to explain or seem to be a gross overreaction occur in schools as a result of a student's hypersensitive limbic system. This means the student is susceptible to overreact whenever he or she is overwhelmed. It is also likely that the reaction will be difficult to explain because all the other individuals who maintain chemical balance will be experiencing a different reality.

The goal of crisis prevention is to allow for reduced stimuli that are likely to be misinterpreted during heightened periods of stress and sufficient time for chemical secretion to return to more normal levels. It is important to remember that for more fragile individuals, the reduction of negative stimuli might need to be in place for up to two days because of their increased sensitivity.

However, the most important goal of crisis prevention is to promote positive perceptions that will induce positive chemical responses, therefore reducing the occurrence of misperception by a hypersensitive limbic system. This can be achieved through a low-stress environment that actively promotes targeted positive perceptions. Low-stress environments that provide for safety, the basic need of the amygdala, reduce the occurrence of violence and conflict.

CHAPTER 5

Understanding the Mind of a Bully

Bullying at its core is an act of fear committed by the weakest among us.
– Horacio Sanchez

A common trigger of crisis situations in schools is bullying. Many of the major catastrophes that have occurred in schools in the past decade were a result of the stress created by students who were being systematically victimized. Under duress, survival instincts kicked in. Adolescents with limited or predominately negative experiences make very poor decisions when they feel that they are backed into a corner. A better understanding of bullying behavior will illustrate the importance of prevention.

Exposure to violence and abuse has long been linked to the occurrence of behaviors such as aggression and bullying. What has not been explored until recently is the impact that this exposure has on brain development. By understanding what happens in the brain and why, educators can take steps to prevent bullying and assist the bully in adopting more socially acceptable behavior.

Let's once again review the important role of the amygdala in order to comprehend its part in bullying behavior. The amygdala, an important part of the limbic system in the brain, is in charge of personal behavioral responses. Any stimulus encountered by an individual is filtered through the amygdala in order for it to assess if the stimulus poses a threat. When the amygdala perceives danger, it will configure a chemical response designed to respond to the situation and release the necessary chemicals into the bloodstream. By releasing the response through the circulatory system, the amygdala seizes control of the body in order to ensure immediate response. The amygdala reduces input from the cortex, which is in charge of reasoning and planning, in direct proportion to the level of the perceived danger. A primary function of the cortex is to provide related data to the amygdala in order to produce a more thoughtful, rational response. However, since the amygdala's role is to ensure survival, if the threat is perceived to be immediate, it will block input from the cortex in order to expedite the "survival" response. Simply put, the more immediate and severe the threat, the lower the percentage of input from the cortex.

The types of personal behavioral responses produced are directly correlated to the past emotional experiences to which an individual has been exposed. The chemical configurations designed by the amygdala to deal with these responses are then stored for faster response if the individual encounters a similar threat in the future. Remember the example of the alcoholic father sexually abusing his son? The response of John's amygdala will become quicker each time he is threatened by his drunken father. Repetitive trauma results not only in a hypersensitive limbic system but also in setting up a predictable pattern of response. A hypersensitive limbic response occurs when the response designed and stored by the amygdala is so repeatedly produced that it can be prematurely released in times of perceived stress, without the related trigger actually being present. Therefore, the response is not one that is rational for the situation but is predictable for this profiled individual when under stress. It is the lack of predictability in students with overly sensitive limbic systems that makes them so challenging in the school setting.

Understanding how the limbic system works makes it logical that the profile of a habitual bully is that of an individual who has been exposed to violence and has been a victim of systematic physical abuse. One might wonder why some people exposed to violence and abuse become timid and withdrawn while others aggress. The individual's temperament is predictive of how he or she will naturally react to stimuli. Individuals with a more difficult temperament seem more prone to mimicking behaviors done to them when stressed. Those with more shy and anxious temperaments seem to internalize and withdraw when the stimuli are present. For the habitual bully, aggression toward others initiates whenever he or she experiences stress. In this context, stress is defined as any stimulus that causes dramatic chemical shifts in the brain. Each individual's emotional health, then, determines how the individual will interpret and react to stress. Victims of systematic abuse often misperceive common everyday occurrences as threatening whenever they become overly stimulated.

The early pattern for the habitual bully is further solidified by the role of mirror neurons and microsaccades in the brain. Mirror neurons are a subset of neurons in the brain – motor areas that reflect acts performed by others in the observer's brain (Rizzolatti et al. 2006). Mirror neurons help us learn social behaviors that we are constantly exposed to at a deeper level. These neurons not only teach the social patterns but also help the brain predict behavioral reactions of others and influence the replication of the practice. Mirror neurons play a tape of certain behavioral practices to increase the occurrence of the behavior and to enable individuals to predict the responses of others. Constant exposure to bullying behaviors provides the bully with a keen ability to predict response patterns of others when they are threatened. The chronic bully will be more astute in selecting individuals who will react with fear to his or her acts of aggression.

In addition, microsaccades provide the bully with an advanced system for subconsciously monitoring behavior patterns he or she has been consistently exposed to. Microsaccades are fixational eye movements that engender visibility when a person's gaze is fixed (S. Martinez-Conde and S. Macknil, 2007, pp. 56–63). They allow humans to scan a wide area and notice subtle changes including nonverbal cues that the amygdala produces. Microsaccades also at a subconscious level identify patterns that are familiar or are objects of attraction. It is likely that the bully will notice subtle behavioral nonverbal cues modeled by individuals who have poor self-esteem and who will likely not fight back when targeted.

However, not all bullies fit the above mentioned profile. There is a range of bullying behavior, and our profile describes individuals who are prone to resort to bullying when feeling threatened or when under stress. Since it is a stress-induced response that reduces thoughtful control, it is best described as a habitual pattern response. Other individuals who are less chemically stable will aggress toward people who are the most different from them when under stress. The amygdala, the part of the brain that is associated with actions such as bullying, is alerted to differences and calmed by commonalities. Individuals suffering from any type of chemical imbalance, whether inherited or produced by stress, tend to be more irritated by that which is different. The distinction between this profile bully and the habitual bully is the lack of victimization and the exposure to violence. Teachers can reduce this type of agitation by always conducting exercises at the beginning of each school year that help students see what they have in common with the other students. This process can be further enhanced by having students work in cooperative groups that are assigned based on things that the students have in common. If teachers manage to have all the students in the class ultimately work with one another during the first few weeks and continually have them recognize that they share things in common, then their amygdalae will be less prone to be agitated by differences. This will dramatically reduce this profile's level of bullying behavior but will not have the same significant level of improvement in the habitual bully.

Bullying behavior also can be engaged in by healthy students in settings where the behavior has become more pervasive. This behavior is caused by the brain's natural tendency to mimic common practices of individuals with whom one identifies. This profile of bullying is the easiest to extinguish because it is not based on a preexisting chemical imbalance or ongoing stress. However, since schools deal with all these profiles simultaneously, they tend to be misled by the success of interventions that have proven successful with only the healthiest profiles. Unless schools are willing to engage in the practices that target the most severe forms of the problem, they will be unable to successfully reduce the behavior in places where it is a significant problem. Since the issues at the more severe levels have to do with chemical imbalance, then the most legitimate plan to address bullying must improve chemical functioning.

The arousal level of the amygdala can be lowered in situations in which there exists a perception of being safe, wanted, and successful. When experiencing these types of emotions, the amygdala perceives stimuli accurately and continues to receive input from the cortex. Since many bullies suffer from poor self-esteem and poor social skills, their level of anxiety often elevates when they are in group settings. In settings like school, bullies experience failure, don't feel wanted, and don't feel safe. Their perceptions lead to a classic catch-22 cycle of aggression: The bully seeks acceptance; earlier life traumas have created atypical response patterns; feeling different from the other students, he or she becomes anxious, leading to acts of aggression. This cycle continues, increasing feelings of isolation and leading to repetitive acts of aggression. Since at the core, bullies are anxious and insecure individuals, it will be natural for them to select victims that they perceive as weaker than themselves.

Schools must make a priority of preventing bullying. The most serious outcome of persistent victimization can be violence. The Institute for Violence Prevention and Criminology in Berlin profiled perpetrators of school rampage killings (as discussed in Roberts 2007, p. 54). The most persistent profile was the shy and anxious temperament student with poor self-esteem and social skills. These students perceived themselves to be perpetual victims of bullying. They retreated into a fantasy world in which they would seek retribution on those who treated them unjustly. They identified with other students who had committed rampage killings, saturated themselves in movies, games, and videos to visualize violent acts, which enabled them to embellish their fantasies. Under the right level of perceived threat, their amygdalae produced violent actions. It is important to remember that bullying can produce violent responses in students who would not have been aggressive under less stressful circumstances.

Once the pattern of school failure is established, school itself will produce increased anxiety and lead to aggressive behaviors. This speaks to the complexity of the issue for the habitual bully. He or she needs to experience success at school as part of a good prevention strategy. It is not surprising that bullying usually occurs in the least structured parts of the school day since the behavior is triggered by chemical arousal. The increased stimuli experienced during all the major transitions become the usual times for these threatening behaviors to escalate: admission to school in the morning, transitions between classes, lunchtime, and dismissal.

To break the cycle of bullying, schools need to establish predictable routines and rituals that aid in lowering the bully's level of anxiety. This means that the initial strategy for lowering persistent bullying is creating predictable school climates that are void of punitive tension. In addition, schools that help students feel successful and wanted will lower the arousal level of the amygdalae, thereby reducing impulsivity. Criminologists have known for decades that building and maintaining strong relationships with bullies or those prone to acts of rage is the best way to prevent violence.

CHAPTER 6

The Central Role of Relationship in Education and Treatment

No significant learning occurs without a significant relationship.
– Dr. James Comer

The ability for schools to begin to successfully promote the perceptions that students are safe, wanted, and can be successful is intricately linked to the concept of *relationship*. The perception of positive nurturing relationships plays an essential role in the ability of the human brain to believe in the existence of the three values of the amygdala mentioned above.

The initial relationship in life – that between the infant and the parent figure – has long-term ramifications for a child's overall development, especially in the area of social skills. This parent figure normally provides structure and stability, creating a predictable environment that denotes safety and security for the infant. In that safe environment, early forms of emotional intelligence begin to formulate. That same sense of safety also correlates to language development and even to advanced social skills such as empathy. However, the presence of multiple risk factors at this juncture can negatively impact social development.

All risk factors seem to impact the quality and consistency of relationships. However, some risk factors are directly correlated to the quality of the parent-child relationship as well as to the quality of the family support network. Three of the early developmental risk factors highlight the significance of the parent-child relationship. These factors are problems in infant-mother attachment, long-term absence from the caregiver, and the birth of other siblings within a two-year period.

Infant-mother attachment refers to the natural act of bonding that occurs between infant and mother in the period soon after birth. It is best described as an intuitive act that occurs within the early weeks following birth. The human mind seems to be predetermined toward attachment to a primary caregiver, and chemical reactions that occur in the body seem to assist in this process. At the time of birth, the hormone oxytocin is elevated in the systems of mother, father, and child. Oxytocin plays a role in initial bonding and in all subsequent relationships. When oxytocin is elevated in the body, stress is reduced, allowing the individual to be calmer and therefore better able to trust.

Oxytocin is triggered in one's system by acts of nurturance, sexual arousal, physical touch, and melodic sounds (Uvnas-Moberg 1997, pp. 146–63). Commonly practiced child-rearing rituals, found in traditional child-parenting acts, seem to trigger oxytocin on a consistent basis. The acts of feeding, holding, massaging, singing, reading, and playing music induce higher levels of oxytocin, insulating many children from the negative impact that stress hormones can have on development. It could be said that relationship is nature's stress regulator. Therefore, it is not surprising that many parents report experiencing a reduction in their own stress when interacting with their babies.

Oxytocin continues to play a role in our parenting, in our other relationships, and in our social memory. In many ways, the rituals practiced during the infant-mother bonding are evidenced in later mating rituals. Many individuals go out to dinner or cook meals for those to whom they are attracted, inducing oxytocin. We utilize melodic tunes in the mating rituals. We engage in foreplay that involves touch. All these actions can trigger oxytocin and reduce inhibitions, thereby increasing feelings of trust. Recognizing the importance of these rituals in later stages of our lives might help explain why the initial relationship between the child and the mother in infancy is so predictive of the quality of future relationships. Those who bond with their parents usually mimic social practices that increase oxytocin in social situations throughout adolescence and into adulthood.

After infant-mother attachment, two other factors have the potential to become early developmental risk factors if not present, both indicating the importance of continued bonding between the parent figure and child. The long-term absence of a main care provider indicates the ongoing importance of continued bonding throughout the developmental stages of a child's life. The presence of a consistent nurturing figure positively impacts social, emotional, and neurological development. Infants count on that person to whom they are bonded to provide consistent verbal, physical, and environmental feedback. In addition, the birth of siblings within a two-year period further emphasizes the importance of having at least one parent who consistently provides nurturance and guidance. Many individuals have siblings born within two years and never view this as a deficit or risk. However, the negative impact of any risk factor is most pronounced in the presence of other risk factors. For example, having a sibling born within a two-year period would not likely impact a healthy child with fewer than two risk factors present in his or her life who is born to healthy parents. However, a child with difficult infant temperament, born to parents with difficulty organizing and structuring a household, might feel the impact of an additional sibling through the loss of attention or in decreased supervision. The increase in the child's level of stress, coupled with the child's temperament, could lead to a misperception of the parents' true level of love and caring. It is important to note that the presence of any early stressor that is constant can lead to a significant change in brain and body chemistry, resulting in unhealthy behaviors.

The implications of relationship for education and treatment have been well documented (Birch and Ladd 1997, 61–79). Both Harvard and Stanford universities conducted longitudinal studies in order to identify the in-school indicators of academic achievement. The studies looked at in-school indicators that were consistent across all student populations. Although several indicators were found to be significant, only one indicator was found to be statistically significant across all student groups. Both studies determined that the perceived quality of the student-teacher relationship had a direct correlation to improved student behavior and academic achievement.

This finding can be explained easily through brain science. The earlier section on crisis illustrated how the perception of stress reduced input from the cortex. During a perceived threat, the adrenal glands immediately release adrenaline. If the threat is severe or still persists after a couple of minutes, the adrenal glands then release cortisol. Once in the brain, cortisol remains much longer than adrenaline, where it continues to affect brain cells. Persistent exposure to elevated levels of cortisol is associated with fearfulness, impaired physical development, hypervigilance, poor emotional intelligence, depression, psychopathologies, impaired declarative memory, and hippocampal damage. When individuals are in the presence of a positive adult relationship, the hormone oxytocin is secreted into the system, thereby mitigating cortisol. When stress is mitigated, the cortex, which is involved in declarative learning, remains engaged.

Consistent, positive adult relationships, therefore, are a natural stabilizer for the body and brain. Corticotropin-releasing hormone (CRH) is triggered in the brain by negative stressful life events, neglect, and the lack of long-term positive nurturance. CRH impacts not only the memory of the cortex but also that of the hippocampus. It is clear that cortisol has direct implications on academic performance. Its impact on the hippocampus slows learning and reduces the accurate filing of what has been learned. Impaired filing means that even though the information has been learned, it will be difficult to retrieve when needed. In addition, the executive functions of the cortex will be reduced and at times inoperable. This means that the student will be less able to apply higher-level skills to solving academic problems.

In addition to lowering cognitive performance, stress impacts human behavior. Stress triggers the blocking or the overproduction of the brain's chemical system, causing surges that are correlated to negative brain function. Stress increases a class of steroids called glucocorticoids in the bloodstream. Glucocorticoids are toxic to the brain. When stress becomes chronic, cell regeneration stops, dendrites disappear, and the hippocampus in charge of learning and memory begins to wither (Lehrer 2006, pp. 59–67.) Children and adolescents have lower activity in their frontal lobes than adults because their cortexes are not fully developed until they are in their early twenties. Persistent exposure to stress can result in a poorly developed prefrontal cortex. It is the prefrontal cortex that enables adolescents to exhibit more thoughtful and controlled responses to life situations. Studies conducted over the last decade have revealed that the cerebral cortexes of teenagers are undergoing dramatic change. Neurotransmitters are radically transforming, creating a desire for risk-taking experiences (McAuliffe 2007, pp. 9–11). That is because new connections are being formed between centers of higher conceptual thinking. Therefore, in the first and second years of high school, students are extremely vulnerable to stress and incidents of poor decision making. Schools that prioritize the development of positive relationships between teachers and students find that they can mitigate the occurrences of such negative incidents.

Relationship is nature's natural regulator for stress. When the hormone oxytocin is released in the presence of positive nurturing relationships, all related stress hormone secretion levels automatically decrease. Several studies found that students consistently performed at a higher level in classes in which they perceived a positive relationship with the teacher (Battistich et al. 1995, pp. 627–58; Shouse 1996, pp. 47–68; Solomon et al. 2000, pp. 3–51; Felner et al. 1997, 528–32 and 541–50). It is interesting to note that the findings were consistent across subject matter, even if the subject was not one that the student had traditionally done well in.

In 1998, I studied an intensive one-to-one reading program that was administered to students who were three or more years behind in reading, had histories of school failure and behavioral problems. Batteries of reading tests were administered to establish baseline scores in a wide range of reading functions. Reading specialists either selected the most appropriate reading program for each student or designed a particular approach, utilizing strategies from several reading programs. Identified students received one hour of one-to-one reading instruction five days a week for one year.

Quarterly, students were administered standardized reading tests and a relationship assessment. The reading tests charted the reading progress of each student. The relationship assessment, which was completed by both teacher and student independently, determined the level of interpersonal connection between student and teacher. All students enrolled in the reading program made at least two grade-level gains in reading based on pre- and posttesting per year. However, the students who advanced three or more levels in reading performance all had only one consistent indicator: they were the students who scored the highest on the relationship assessment.

A comprehensive study on mental health treatment was undertaken in order to determine what constitutes effective mental health care. The study looked at a wide range of presenting problems, treatment approaches, and specific service configurations. The study found no service or treatment approach more effective than another for treating individuals suffering from chronic mental health issues. However, the study did determine that what seemed most predictive of service success was the quality of the relationship the client had with family and peers. Also, the existence of long-term positive relationships serves as a catalyst for the development of protective factors that diminish the presence of risk. The study concluded that "successful interventions with adolescents with aggressive disorders may require building social support bridges to estranged families or friends" (Vance et al. 2002).

Therefore, relationship must be viewed as a central emphasis for effective education. Schools must find or create effective ways to improve the relationships between teachers and the children or adolescents whom they instruct.

CHAPTER 7

Using What We Know about Relationship to Improve Education

If you improve education by teaching for competence, eliminating schooling, and connecting with students, the test scores will improve.

– William Glasser

The problem is that many of the individuals who are most in need of *relationship* are the same individuals who already have demonstrated problems in identifying and maintaining positive long-term relationships. Therefore, schools should seek to implement formal or informal mentoring programs for the students most in need. Schools have a long tradition of providing informal mentoring to students. Many a teacher has taken a special interest in a particular student, which contributed to his or her ability to stay in school and achieve more than was expected. However, since neurobiology has revealed the important role that relationship plays in behavior and learning, it is imperative that schools become more focused on this approach.

Informal mentoring programs can be established as easily as nominating students at each staff meeting and having teachers volunteer to meet the established requirements of a mentor. The requirements can be outlined as minimal amounts of contacts, accompanying students when they must deal with a problem, and making recommendations that might help the student become more successful. Formal mentor programs seek to match students with the appropriate role model, determine contact hours based on level of need, and identify specific areas to work on.

Many students who have not experienced positive social relationships can become guarded in all future social interactions. They are usually lacking in social skills that are developed over time through daily positive social interactions. Mentorship is a natural model for the development of social skills through real daily interaction and practice.

Knowing what brain science teaches us about relationships helps us understand not only why mentorship works but also what has to be done to make it consistent and effective. Mentors must continually remind themselves that attempts to buffer, sabotage, and even end any relationship have to do with the nature of the pathology and not with them personally. As a result, mentors must continually engage in practices that promote social bonding and lead to the acceptance of mentorship. Since stress is one of the main obstacles to relationship building, rituals and practices should be quickly established and faithfully adhered to so that social interaction can be predictable and practiced daily.

Mentorship works because human beings are biologically predisposed to benefit from long-term positive relationships. The hormone oxytocin is secreted in the body and the brain during positive social interaction. Since oxytocin is required for body development, emotional stability, and learning, the absence of consistent secretions of this hormone is correlated to stunted body development, increased emotional disorders, and cognitive impairment.

We must ensure that mentors know just how important their behaviors are in teaching students with whom they work. The emphasis on modeling desired behaviors is based on the law of isopraxism, which states that what is consistently modeled before us is most likely to impact behavior (Givens 2005). Almost everyone who becomes a parent can attest to the realization that regardless of cognitive decisions to parent differently from their parents, most repeat the parenting practices that they experienced. Teachers also discover that they teach for the most part as they were taught, and best friends become aware that they have begun to model similar behaviors. However, there are some factors that must be present before the law of isopraxism takes effect; there must be identification with the individual modeling the behavior and the person witnessing the behavior. The behavior must be modeled consistently, and the behavior itself must become an action that is chemically reinforced in the brain.

The ultimate goal of the mentoring relationship is to bring about long-term change by teaching new behaviors in a manner that is most natural to the human brain. That is because modeling is the most natural form of instruction to the brain. The most significant factor impeding this process is that cognitive understanding is not correlated to behavioral change. Mentors must be taught the scientific process of change; they must understand what has to occur in the brain in order for someone to incorporate what is being taught in a way that makes initial change and then long-term change possible.

Understanding the role of the amygdala in our behavior is critical to understanding why students behave as they do. It is imperative that individuals engaged in mentoring constantly be reminded that only the most emotionally significant things learned and experienced are available to all individuals in times of crisis. Therefore, individuals who are void of many positive emotional lessons and experiences cannot be expected to produce these types of behaviors when stressed. Knowing this helps us understand why rational, intelligent individuals in times of high stress are capable of actions counter to both their character and intellectual capacity.

The role of the amygdala in learning and behavior clearly illustrates the importance of mentorship. The amygdala automatically registers and analyzes any social cue used by humans to demonstrate emotion, such as facial expression, body posture, gestures, hand movements, and tone of voice. This monitoring of emotional expressions plays a vital role in survival. During strong emotions, the chemicals released by the amygdala produce certain facial expressions, body postures, gestures, and voice tones. That is why certain gestures such as a shoulder shrug, facial expressions such as the wrinkling of the eyebrows, or the increase in pitch of the tone of voice occur across cultures, sexes, and races in the presence of certain external stimuli. The reality is that lessons taught in a brain-based manner are often enhanced in the amygdala when they are learned in the context of a significant relationship. This happens because the amygdala is hardwired to focus on the nonverbal cues that humans produce.

This automated level of focus on nonverbal cues gives human interaction a place of emphasis in the human brain. Mentors should be taught how the amygdala works and how to utilize techniques that increase amygdala response during interventions. For example, when working with a student who is escalating, a mentor should know what facial expression, body posture, and tone of voice to use that would be interpreted by the amygdala as safe. The role of the mentor is to take advantage of daily situations to teach important life lessons. Lessons learned in the context of a significant relationship are more likely to be held in the amygdala since there are so many facets of human interaction that the amygdala is hardwired to focus on. Not only the amygdala will automatically focus on the nonverbal cues produced by another person, but also the amygdala will value anything done that is associated with caring. That is why significant relationships have had such a strong impact on shaping new behaviors.

Once a new behavior is initiated, the goal is to make sure it is not quickly extinguished. In order to become a consistent practice, a behavior requires reinforcement in the brain. The act of reinforcement occurs in another portion of the limbic system called the nucleus accumbens. The nucleus accumbens undergoes a shift in dopamine level during all persistent behaviors. Dopamine shifts in this region of the brain were first documented in primary behaviors such as eating, drinking, and sexual intercourse. Later these shifts were identified to occur in chemical addictions. Due to the advancements in brain science, it is now known that all habitual or persistent behaviors require a shift in dopamine levels in the nucleus accumbens. For applied learning or behavioral change to become habitual, information must stimulate the prefrontal cortex and the amygdala, triggering a predopamine shift that is predictive of activation of the nucleus accumbens. If this shift occurs, the nucleus accumbens will begin to see the act itself as rewarding and continue to trigger dopamine shifts whenever the applied learning or behavioral change occurs.

What has been learned about the nucleus accumbens dictates that the most efficient way to trigger the desired chemical shift is to ensure that the desired behavior is learned in the context of a significant relationship. This means that the release of oxytocin stimulates the nucleus accumbens, which then triggers the reward pathway that allows for conditioning and learning (Uvnas-Moberg 1998, pp. 819–35). In addition, it has been discovered that the probability for chemical reinforcement in the brain is increased when the behavior is reinforced externally by a significant other. External reinforcement is more likely to be recognized by the brain as a reward when the brain can consistently predict the occurrence and when the external reward is accompanied by certain brain-based components such as facial expressions, gestures, touch, and voice tones that have already been interpreted by the amygdala as positive or valuable.

CHAPTER 8

Climate

Students cannot learn well and are not likely to behave well in difficult school environments.

– Dr. James P. Comer

S chools must consider creating positive climates before attempting to implement a behavioral modification program. A positive climate can reduce stress, therefore improving learning and behavioral performance. McEwen found that chronic stress reduces the length and braiding of dendrites in the brain's medial prefrontal cortex by about 20 percent (Lambert and Lilienfeld 2007, p. 52). This dendrite reduction in turn reduces focus, learning of new information, and long-term memory. In addition, a stressful environment will not allow any programmatic services, teaching strategies, or behavioral interventions to have the opportunity to be implemented effectively. Research by Zins and Ponti concerning implementation of new programs within schools revealed that regardless of the quality of the program itself, success was intricately dependent on the overall health of the school climate: "Effective programs cannot survive in difficult school climates" (Zins and Ponti 1990).

The need for a positive environmental climate begins at the time one is born and continues to the end of life. The lack of a predictable nurturing environment can be one of the most devastating circumstances for an infant's brain and body development. Predictable environments lessen negative hormone secretions in the brain. Less stress improves the occurrence of infant-mother attachment and enables learning. Predictable environments are so critical to child development that the brain of a mother is prewired to ritualize feeding patterns and sleeping patterns. Healthy mothers seem to interpret the infant's nonverbal cues in order to develop an appropriate feeding and sleeping schedule. This simple process is crucial in preventing early stress, emotional disorders, and physical problems.

Infants who cannot adopt a consistent sleeping and eating pattern are at greater risk of developing physical and emotional problems. Predictability, especially related to eating and sleeping, activates the brain's reward system by triggering the midbrain dopaminergic neurons. This triggering begins to establish the crucial pathway known as the nucleus accumbens (the reward pathway). This pathway is crucial because it is now known that behavioral anomalies such as conduct disorder, antisocial personality disorder, and all forms of addictions are related to an inoperative reward pathway. Researchers Blum, Cull, Braverman, and Comings refer to it as reward deficiency syndrome (RDS). They found that a common genetic deficiency in the dopamine D2 receptors resulted in the brain's inability to reinforce daily activities that most people find rewarding (Blum et al. 1996, pp.132–145). This inability to experience pleasure in daily activities seems to lead to more extreme behaviors in order to stimulate dopamine D2 activity in the brain. This same region of the brain is responsible for eating and sleeping patterns. When the reward pathway does not function normally, a disturbance in eating and sleeping patterns usually follows. The disturbance of eating and sleeping patterns predicts future problems in one's ability to conform to life's demands that require discipline. This means these individuals will struggle with simple routines such as homework.

Individuals who are at greater risk for developing RDS are those born with chemical imbalance in the brain, difficult or anxious temperaments, or those exposed early to stressful environments void of predictable rules, routines, and rituals. The conclusion is that humans require anchor points for healthy development. Life's common anchor points are waking up, the main meal of the day, and bedtime. Healthy climates promote predictable routines that aid in balanced brain chemistry and a healthy, active nucleus accumbens.

It is not surprising to learn that for many individuals found to be resilient, schools were identified as the environments that promoted stabilized brain chemistry and an active reward pathway (Werner 2000, pp. 97–116). It seems that schools also have anchor points: admission, lunch, and dismissal. Schools that establish consistent rituals for these major transitions seem to have better outcomes. School anchor points seem to mimic the anchor points provided in the home: wake-up, main meal, and bedtime rituals. Homes that produce better outcomes with all children provide safe and orderly climates that minimize the stress that a major transition can produce. Schools also can produce better outcomes for students by establishing ritualized climates. The participation in consistent transition rituals activates the reward pathway by promoting a positive perception about the school that is able to be internalized by students.

How are orderly transitions and positive perceptions best achieved? The reason that transitions are so predictive of how an environment will be perceived is that all transitions increase chemical activity in the brain. That is because all sensory processing results in chemical activity. Transitions increase the amount of sensory activity that is processed at any given time. The more activity there is in an environment, the more chemical activity there will be in the brain. For individuals suffering from chemical imbalance in the brain, the additional chemical activity produced by the processing of crowds, noise, odors, and movements can result in overstimulation and impulsive behaviors. That is why individuals who suffer from behavioral disorders usually have a higher rate of incidents during all the major transitions in the school day.

Since children encounter so many stressors in their lives, it is not uncommon for incidents that take place outside of school to be the source of heightened levels of anxiety that produce inappropriate responses to stimuli. Students under stress are more susceptible to becoming chemically overwhelmed and impulsive. There are two basic methods for improving major transitions in the school day. One can reduce stimuli or one can ritualize practices. The reduction of stimuli is easy to explain. By reducing what the brain has to process, we can reduce the amount of chemical activity. Schools often have at their disposal various methods for reducing stimuli. Many schools have numerous entrances and exits. Desiring to improve supervision, schools often funnel all students through one entrance or exit point. It would be better to have students assigned different entry points if doing so can reduce how far they will travel and the number of other students they have to encounter. This approach allows each student to process only the movement in just one portion of the school building. In addition, schools can stagger transitions throughout the school day and drastically reduce the stimuli in the hallways. By having different groups of students leave and arrive at their classes in staggered five-minute intervals, a school can reduce the number of students moving at any one time. This type of scheduling takes additional planning, but the investment in time is well worth the reduction of incidents throughout the school year.

Many transitions during the school day are initiated by a loud school bell or buzzer. The emotional brain, the amygdala, is alerted by loud, startling sound. By alerting the amygdala, schools are alerting the part of the brain responsible for emotional behavior and impulsive actions. Schools should seek to trigger transitions with more rhythmic tones. This will not alert the amygdala prior to every transition. Schools can determine the rhythmic pattern they want students to transition to by incorporating appropriate music to influence the body's heart and blood rate. By influencing the body's heart and blood rate, one essentially can slow or speed up the rate of physical movement. Schools should seek to play music that is sixty beats per measure in the background throughout the transition. The music can denote the beginning of the class change, and a change in tone could signal that there are only sixty seconds before students will be counted as tardy.

Schools also can attempt to ritualize these transitions. By having certain elements in the transition occur consistently every day, the brain will grow accustomed to the process, therefore lowering the alertness of the amygdala. The amygdala is alerted to things that are different because they pose a threat. Many schools think that they already have transition rituals in place because they have a schedule. However, the human brain requires that other elements be part of a ritual in order that it not dramatically increase chemical activity.

Schools can teach specific rituals for the major transitions in the school day. For example, students can be taught always to transition on the right side of the halls, always walk, and keep their hands and feet to themselves. The student is consistently told that just achieving these three steps means that their school days will all go better. The additional sensory component of playing music in the background to influence the pace of the transition adds to the ability of the brain to recognize the pattern. Moreover, schools should provide adequate supervision during all transitions. Transitions should have only a few identified rules, but we must insist that all the adults in the school consistently model and reinforce these practices. The neurobiological importance of the modeling and consistent participation in established rituals by the adults involved is addressed later in this book.

A positive perception of school climate is best achieved by aligning the sensory ritual to one or more of the three universal positive perceptions: you are safe, you are wanted, and you can be successful. The following is a brief explanation of what is required for a ritual to be reinforced by the human brain. A more detailed explanation will come later in the chapter on the reward pathway. A sensory ritual is required because the process needs to stimulate the prefrontal cortex, the hippocampus, and the amygdala in order to activate the reward pathway. The prefrontal cortex registers learning that stimulates the senses. It is also responsible for motivating new behaviors. The unique feature of the prefrontal cortex is that it can stimulate dopamine secretions associated with the reward pathway. This stimulation requires a visual cue that is consistently associated with a practice that has at one time received chemical reinforcement in the nucleus accumbens. For example, a heroin addict consistently uses a spoon to prepare the drug before shooting up. The chemical enters the brain and is perceived to be dopamine and is in itself reinforcing. After the repetitive practice is established, the prefrontal cortex needs only to see the spoon in order to secrete a type of dopamine associated with motivation. In the case of addiction, the motivation will create a craving strong enough to promote the associated action. This example clearly illustrates why identifying a symbolic cue can be so effective for triggering a desired behavior. This is also why advertisers spend millions of dollars establishing logos that they hope will trigger a behavior such as drinking a particular soft drink.

The limbic system, the hippocampus, and the amygdala are the areas in the brain where strong beliefs, emotional responses, and habitual behaviors originate. The hippocampus is where learning is initiated. The hippocampus registers everything processed through the senses and retains memory for an average of two weeks but will store sensory input related to a strong emotional event. This part of the limbic system is highly involved in procedural learning and repetitive procedures that involve high sensory activity. The hippocampus does not retain language long-term unless it is attached to high sensory input. As a result, behaviors that are likely to be stored in the hippocampus are those procedural activities that involve multiple senses and the prefrontal cortex or those events that produce high levels of emotions tied to the senses through the amygdala. Therefore, in order for a behavior or information to be learned, recalled in times of crisis, and become persistent, it must be taught in a specific procedural manner that involves multiple senses. This is why the military trains personnel by having them perform, under induced emotional stress, behavioral sequences that are tied to their survival.

The amygdala stores highly emotional events and relies on the hippocampus for related sensory data recorded during the event. The prefrontal cortex does not supply information during situations producing extreme emotion. The amygdala, even in extreme emotional periods, limits information from the hippocampus and relies on a small bank of stored sensory data held in times of trauma and euphoria. The key to changing extreme behavior is to teach to the amygdala. This can be achieved by aligning a universal perception in the amygdala to a sensory-stimulated procedure that is also symbolically recognized in the prefrontal cortex. When all the above systems work in concert, the likelihood that D2 dopamine will be secreted in the reward pathway is increased.

The reward pathway is the source of all persistent behavior. No behavior consistently occurs unless it is somehow reinforced by dopamine. The role of the reward pathway was first thought to be activated during behaviors that are related to survival such as eating, drinking, and sex. Later studies on addiction revealed that the reward pathway is involved in all chemical addictions. Recent brain imagery revealed that activity in the reward pathway also occurs whenever someone engages in any daily routine, no matter how mundane. Man's ability to engage in any consistent behavior, be persistent in achieving a goal, or maintain a new behavior requires reinforcement in the reward pathway. The reward pathway responds to highly charged emotional and sensory input, to chemical surges that resemble dopamine, and to predictable sensory procedures that are valued by the amygdala.

It is unlikely that schools can create emotionally charged events that can be strategically aligned to desired behavioral practices and learning. However, they can establish ritualized patterns and maintain a disciplined manner in order to forge new, persistent behaviors.

Steps to Developing a New, Persistent Practice That Is the Cornerstone of Establishing Positive Climates

Hippocampus

- Establish a sensory procedure.

Amygdala

- Align sensory procedure to universal emotion.
  - Need to be safe
  - Need to be wanted
  - Need to be successful

- Model desired practice.
  - The law of isopraxism

Prefrontal Cortex

- Establish a visual cue.

Nucleus Accumbens

- Maintain predictable, persistent practice.
- Occasionally recognize and tangibly reinforce.
  - Novelty and recognition can trigger the nucleus accumbens.

CHAPTER 9

Language

Think like a wise man but communicate in the language of the people.
– William Butler Yeats

It has been established that language processing is reduced whenever chemical imbalance occurs. Since instruction in Western culture is predominately delivered and evaluated through language-based methods, it is important that schools address issues surrounding language. In 1991, Lieberman determined that language is only two hundred thousand to a million years old (pp. 63–65). Verbal language was not recorded until the late fourth millennium BC – Cuneiform script began as a system of pictographs (Cooper 1973, pp. 239–246). The questions are challenging: How did man communicate prior to the inception of language, and how did the brain change in order to accommodate the production of speech, reading, and writing?

Inherent mechanisms of communication significantly predate the occurrence of language. It is not surprising that the innate communication system in the brain is located in the section known as the "primitive brain" (the limbic system). One of the functions of the amygdala is to interpret the intentions of man through nonverbal mechanisms. Since the inception of language, the amygdala's function in communication often has been subconscious but is never inoperative. Man's dependence on language has resulted in his lack of conscious awareness of the significant role the amygdala plays in all communication. For example, the amygdala aids language by interpreting nonverbal cues such as facial expressions. A simple expression such as "That is a lovely dress you are wearing" can be given a range of meaning through the amygdala. With a condescending look, "That is a lovely dress you are wearing" would be interpreted as sarcasm; with a look of adoration, it would be a compliment; and with a flat affect, it would be interpreted as merely being polite.

Regardless of the continued evolution of language, man's nonverbal system remains intricately involved in meaning and interpretation. This nonverbal system allowed man to communicate strong emotions, develop nonverbal cues among clans, and even develop long-distance signaling systems. All this was accomplished prior to the development of formal language.

There are many theories about the first development of language. The theory most accepted by anthropologists and scientists who study the brain is related to man's natural proclivity for object focus (Fried et al. 1997, pp. 753–65). Many anthropologists have proposed that man's tendency to focus on objects and to find usefulness in them led to the development of tools and then to the labeling of those objects. Many scientists who study the brain support this theory since the amygdala naturally focuses on objects that are associated with value or emotion. Therefore, language most likely developed from man's need to label possessions.

It is clear that the brain rewired in order to accommodate language. The basal ganglia rewired later in brain evolution to help produce human speech and syntax (Lieberman 1991, pp. 106–07). Somehow, no language center was ever formed in the brain. Rather, the brain seems to have adapted a wide range of existing brain functions and has them work in concert to produce speech, reading, and writing.

The many processes involved in language acquisition and production create a myriad of problems. The brain requires multiple regions to process stimuli in a millisecond in order to produce meaning. First, this means that all the regions involved need to be functioning optimally. Therefore, individuals suffering from any regional damage involved in language processing would immediately be at a disadvantage. This population would include not only persons with brain injury or damage but also individuals suffering from emotional disorders that are caused by chemical imbalance in a region or regions involved in language processing. We also know that students under persistent stress but who have sufficient cognitive capacity can exhibit language deficiencies. Language systems are very sensitive to chemical imbalance in the brain. Studies have shown that when a person's limbic system is overly stimulated, many brain regions involved in language acquisition fail to function appropriately, leading to impaired hearing, word recognition, and interpretation. If stress can temporarily impact language processing in a healthy brain, it will certainly impact a brain suffering from chemical imbalance.

Some of the brain regions involved in language processing are not fully developed in healthy children until the age of ten. Until that point in development, children use their left extrinsic cortex to process language. The left extrinsic cortex is primarily utilized in the processing of visual stimuli. After repetitive exposure to a formalized language system, the brain shifts from pictorial recognition to a subconscious application of a learned process. As a result, appropriate language development requires exposure to appropriate language during this stage of development in order for the developing brain to accommodate the process. It requires a brain in which the regions involved in language acquisition are functioning normally. It also requires low stress environments as well as low internal perceptions of stress.

Language is always being clarified and refined through any movements, gestures, expressions, and patterns that the brain is hardwired to focus on. For example, students in small math tutorials were more likely to learn new concepts when teachers used gestures that appropriately reinforced their message. The teachers' gestures served not just to direct the students' attention to the numbers in the problem but conveyed problem-solving strategies not directly expressed in speech. A teacher explaining the concept of mathematical equivalence might say, "Both sides of the equation have to be the same," first making flat palm gestures under one side of the equation and then under the other. Children were significantly less likely to learn if the teacher did not gesture or inadvertently used a gesture that did not correspond with her verbal instructions (Latta 2000).

Studies of cohorts from high-risk environments determined that there is a lower language emphasis among these groups (Kaiser and Delaney 1996, pp. 66–85). This is logical since their limbic systems are consistently more engaged. Individuals from high-risk environments are negatively impacted by stress, which produces lower exposure to normative language. When the limbic system is activated, language processing will remain or revert to the left extrinsic function. This would relegate language comprehension back to the same process utilized by children before all the regions of the brain required for language comprehension are fully developed. A child's process for comprehending language is heavily dependent on the utilization of specific nonverbal cues that are made available by the communicant.

Abusive environments pose additional risk to language development. Cognitive and language deficits in abused children have been noted clinically (Augoustinos 1987, pp. 15–27; Azar et al. 1988; Fantuzzo 1990, pp. 316–39; Kolko 1992, pp. 719–27). Abused and neglected children with no evidence of neurological impairment also have shown delayed intellectual development, particularly in the area of verbal intelligence (Augoustinos 1987, pp. 15–27). Some studies have found lowered intellectual functioning and reduced cognitive functioning in abused children (Hoffman-Plotkin and Twentyman 1984, pp. 794–802; Perry et al. 1983, pp. 1297–99). Recent studies on high-risk groups revealed that the damage to the hippocampus produced by stress or trauma manufactures a need for visual cueing or evidence to be present in conjunction with any new concept. Simply put, the brain still requires pictures to process new information.

This finding explains why those in marketing always identify a recognizable logo with any new product targeted at high-risk populations. It also begins to explain why gang affiliation is so strong among at-risk youth. Gangs repetitively align central concepts to sensory rituals that are anchored to symbols. The human brain when under stress is more focused on symbols and more likely to learn concepts that are consistently aligned to a symbol. This anchoring enables the impaired hippocampus to learn and process the new information; it allows the prefrontal cortex to store the memory, and it allows the amygdala to connect a value to the symbol. Gangs engage the amygdalae of the members by stressing that their daily survival is dependant on allegiance, and they anchor that concept to a symbol. So powerful is this technique that thousands of at-risk youth commit violent acts toward others based solely on seeing a symbol associated with a rival gang. In a crude manner, gangs and the media teach to the limbic system, which can induce dopamine in the reward pathway. This approach will not only trigger behaviors but also reinforce these behaviors.

Education must take the required steps to improve language processing for students suffering from chemical imbalances. Schools must determine to focus on establishing ritualized climates as the foundation of closing the achievement gap. In addition, language can be better learned and processed by the utilization of brain-based strategies and the consistent emphasis on nonverbal cues that the amygdala focuses on to enhance comprehension. Likewise, educational agencies should be very careful in associating language skills to intellect. This association has resulted in many individuals with great capacity going undeveloped because of chemical imbalance and/or limited exposure.

CHAPTER 10

Behaviors

> *Good schools, like good societies and good families,*
> *celebrate and cherish diversity.*
>
> – *Deborah Meier*

S chools are locations where large numbers of individuals are assembled together. These individuals represent a wide range of cultures, backgrounds, and beliefs. Whenever diverse groups are brought together and forced to interact, there will be some conflicts. Schools often claim that their most important charge is to educate, but their number one charge should be to manage human behavior in order for education to occur. Educators must become experts in the field of human behavior, for without a valid understanding of human behavior, they will be less likely to make decisions that will reduce the occurrence of human conflict and allow education to occur.

The purpose of this chapter is not to address behavior management. It is to demonstrate how much of human behavior is a subconscious response toward others. Humans are in a constant level of arousal. We are hardwired to register and even react to certain nonverbal cues. Many of the behaviors that occur in schools are a direct result of nonverbal triggers and the human condition. By the human condition, I mean the individual's level of chemical balance. The lack of awareness of the world of nonverbal communication has resulted in a level of blindness not only to causation of negative behaviors but also to our responsibility to monitor and positively influence the human condition.

Behaviors are products of interactive systems in the brain. Unless one develops a clear understanding of how these systems work and interact, the ability to predict, manage, and change behavior will be virtually impossible. Two primary systems in the brain responsible for producing behaviors are the amygdala and the cortex.

The amygdala is responsible for two major categories of behaviors. The first category is innate. Innate behaviors are best described as actions that are results of predetermined pathways in the brain that will naturally occur if there is appropriate brain function and the appropriate environmental conditions and/or stimuli. Human developmental milestones can be characterized as innate behaviors. Since the brain is not fully developed at birth, nature programs a sequence of pathways to be triggered at the right stage of development by the right stimulus in order to produce a healthy brain. For example, at about three weeks of brain development, a baby is capable of producing a smile. All that is required is a safe environment, a healthy brain, and the correct stimulus. This pathway, which is related to pleasure, becomes one of the most significant pathways for continued brain development. That is why the behavior is programmed to occur so early in life.

The amygdala is also in charge of personal behavioral responses. As mentioned earlier, any stimulus encountered is filtered through the amygdala in order for it to assess if the stimulus is a threat. Since the amygdala's primary role is survival, it stores vital emotional memory at a different speed. This ensures that when a threat is present and the cortex response is slowed or prevented, it can access vital information quickly without "thinking." This is why the amygdala is alerted to anything we encounter that we are not familiar with. The amygdala goes into a state of high arousal and will remain alerted until the situation is deemed safe. This means that whenever a social situation brings groups of people who are not familiar with one another or who do not share external similarities, we should expect a higher rate of arousal leading to the occurrence of emotional behaviors. Schools can predict periods of high arousal: at the beginning of each school year, at the return from vacations, and even at the addition of new students. Schools should seek to bring students from different grade levels in at different times. It is also best to have seniors or the older students take on the responsibility of orientation of freshmen or younger students. This will increase a sense of familiarity between the two most dissimilar groups: those who are older and very familiar with the setting, and those who are younger and unfamiliar with the setting and people. Reducing the amygdala's level of arousal at the point of initial encounter will, in turn, reduce some perception of irritation and threat that often occurs between groups when stress rises.

Since emotional memories are stored at a faster rate of speed, they are accessed by the amygdala first; thus, past traumatic experiences tend to influence crisis the most. That is because traumatic experiences automatically trigger an intricate sensory connection that creates high-speed memories. The problem is that sensory elements related to the event can activate similar behavioral responses when the individual perceives himself or herself under stress. It is important to remember that students who have been constantly exposed to trauma and are under constant stress often produce similar behaviors from their past as a response to crisis during unrelated events. These behavioral explosions can be triggered whenever the individual reaches a high level of arousal. This is what makes these students so unpredictable and why teachers struggle with these students in their classrooms. Once the student has demonstrated a pattern of overreaction to benign stimuli, the teacher will constantly feel stressed or even threatened in the student's presence. The teacher will also become more emotional in response to situations involving the student in the classroom. This level of focus will be interpreted by the student as unfair and even persecuting. Interestingly enough, when that student is not present, the teacher and even the other students in the class will feel chemically better, thus creating a desire on the part of the students and teacher that the student be removed from the class permanently. This is why it is so critical to create environments that improve everyone's chemical disposition. Positive school climates benefit the ability of all students and adults to function at their best.

It is important not to view brain functions as discrete, separate tasks performed by different regions of the brain. All brain functions are interrelated processes in which the stimulus determines the level of integration. All brain functions primarily carried out by a certain brain region always impact another region. Imagine stimuli on a linear scale of arousal: level 1 represents low emotion, while level 5 signifies high emotion. A stimulus rated at a 1 would be considered mild; this means that the cortex will provide a high level of input prior to the amygdala's designing and releasing the chemical response. At level 5, the cortex will be allowed to give very little input before the amygdala configures and releases the chemical response.

Level 5 responses are therefore more instinctive and evaluated based on past emotional experiences that are stored in the amygdala. That is why a teacher having a negative experience with a student in which he or she felt threatened can alter the perception of all future behaviors. It is important to remember that the amygdala stores only highly emotional experiences. An equally important fact is that memories stored by the amygdala are incomplete. The amygdala is highly dependent on the hippocampus for the sensory data and focuses on specific aspects of the event that it related to the chemical surge. For this reason, many aspects of emotional memories are incomplete because it is not global knowledge that helps in evaluation but rather the specific level of arousal caused by the perceived stimulus. For example, during a traumatic experience in the classroom, the identified student was tapping his pencil on the desk prior to the crisis occurring. It would not be uncommon for the amygdala to recall the tapping of the pencil while not recording other pertinent facts. Level 5 responses, then, are never based on a wealth of data that an individual possesses, but rather on the highly emotional stimulus randomly associated with the event, like the tapping of a pencil. We can understand that after weeks of worrying about when the student will again demonstrate the extreme emotional behaviors he did during the initial crisis, the teacher will be more likely to misinterpret the intentions of the same student when he begins to tap his pencil. Constant exposure to extreme negative emotions leads to poor analysis and misinterpretation of stimuli. Man is simply not designed for constant exposure to extreme stress.

The cortex is responsible for producing a range of behaviors that fall into two general categories: learned response and societal response. Learned response is best defined as a low emotional action that has become predictable, expected, and normative. Societal responses have their roots in innate behaviors. Observations indicate that when innate behaviors are consistently produced and noticed by those within a large cohort group, they become an expectation of the group that later become formalized. For example, most social greetings are products of the amygdala's need to feel safe. The amygdala produces innate behaviors that are responses to stimuli. All behavior requires chemical signals in the brain to be sent in order to produce the action. Certain innate behaviors are perceived by the brain to be pleasurable, such as a smile. Over time, man learned that a smile is produced as a response to positive stimuli. Since the amygdala is alerted to differences and recognizes intuitive responses, man incorporated certain signals into the initial encounters with strangers in order to send a clear message that he meant the other no harm.

The greeting ritual evolved to incorporate smile and touch (handshake or hug) to put the amygdala at ease. Now formalized, greeting practices are modeled by parents, taught to children, and are even essential to one's ability to be successful in society. Individuals from high-risk environments also engage in social greetings that relax the amygdala. However, they are less able to do this with individuals they do not identify with. This is due to a higher level of stress heightening their amygdalae's alertness to differences. Those who are at risk often do not feel like they are a part of those in the social norm, producing an inability to participate in accepted nonverbal greeting cues that would help relax the amygdalae of all involved. This simple issue is enough to create sufficient discomfort in the human brain to drive a wedge between the social groups. As a result, individuals from different socioeconomic backgrounds and cultures that are most successful in society are those that can easily adapt and mimic behaviors of those in the social norm or those who are in power. A socially acceptable greeting triggers the chemical signal for "I come in peace." The practices of social greetings speak directly to the primitive brain's ability to be a social creature.

Schools that promote a more uniformed greeting ritual seem to help individuals from different groups feel less threatened. There are two methods for achieving a uniformed social greeting ritual within a school. One is to teach it to all the students. The other is to have it modeled by the adults. The latter has proven more successful. If the adults within an institution consistently model a social greeting ritual, it is very likely that the students will mimic it or develop one of their own. That is because the amygdala is prewired to monitor this behavior and notice it whenever it occurs. This means it will be learned without formally having to be taught and that it will become comforting because it is a familiar pattern associated with a natural value of the primitive brain. The issue that many schools encounter in instituting such a practice is that the adults represent a wide range of socioeconomic backgrounds and cultures. These differences between the adults often prevent a natural occurrence of consistently modeled social greetings among all the school staff. Therefore, schools must seek to institute a more formal practice and teach staff why it is so important.

Man's ability to produce some innate behaviors on demand led to the behavioral pattern known as mixed response. Mixed response is best defined as the conscious triggering or manipulation of learned patterns of the primitive brain. For example, natural laughter was observed to occur when a certain stimulus was encountered in a certain way and at a certain time. Man's ability to manipulate these innate patterns allowed him to create artificial processes and orchestrated stimuli, in which the stimuli would be presented in order to evoke the desired response. Early records of musicians and court jesters give evidence that the ability to trigger or manipulate innate response was valued very early in man's evolution. The importance of this knowledge is evidenced in the continuing growth of the entertainment industry. It is important to note that individuals who share similar experiences have similar mixed response patterns. This is also predictive of why social groupings occur. The amygdala likes seeing itself. When the amygdala notes a response pattern that it shares, it is likely to be drawn to that individual. This further stresses the importance of safe environments in which these attraction patterns don't become a point of clear separation. In a safe setting, the amygdala is more accepting of differences it has had sufficient exposure to. Where individuals have shared similar experiences, both tolerance and the range of attractions will increase. Schools should be safe settings that promote social acceptance.

What all behaviors have in common is at their source is preprogrammed innate chemical response patterns. The awareness that many human response patterns are programmed in the brain came from studies on human responses carried out across genders and cultures. These studies determined that, at certain stages of human development, individuals respond in a similar manner to certain stimuli. For example, children around a certain age all over the world shrug their shoulders when asked a question to indicate "I don't know." Many such prewired behavioral patterns are produced by the amygdala as an external expression to the internal chemical condition.

Not only is there a range of input by the cortex to the amygdala based on the level of arousal, but also there is also a range of intensity in relation to innate behaviors. The nature of the innate behavioral response is determined also by the level of arousal. For example, the higher the emotional signal, the more dramatic the physical response, the less conscious one will be of the response, and the lower the ability to mask the response. Moreover, since the amygdala releases the chemical response that produces these reaction patterns, it is also subconsciously able to interpret the meaning of external expressions it is hardwired to produce. Many individuals have experienced meeting someone for the first time and immediately not liking or trusting him/her. This feeling is usually the result of the individual's amygdala subconsciously detecting some innate behavioral cue that previously has been interpreted as negative.

Scientists have identified the physical responses that are controlled by the amygdala. If teachers and administrators become more aware of these physical signs, they will become more able to act in a preventive manner. The amygdala can seize control of the face, hands, voice tone, body movements, and postures. The face constitutes the most highly differentiated and versatile set of neuromuscular mechanisms in man. It reflects at least nine major emotions: interest, enjoyment, surprise, distress, anger, shame, fear, and contempt. In response to a perceived stimulus, the amygdala signals the nerve nucleus in the brain stem to produce certain facial responses. The more intense the perceived stimulus, the more the amygdala seizes control of facial expressions.

Since it takes identified chemicals in the brain to produce a facial expression, a change in facial expression can impact mood. A study conducted by Davis and Palladino showed the impact of facial expression on mood and behavior (Davis and Palladino 2002). Two groups of participants were shown a sequence of funny cartoons. One group was forced to hold a pencil between their lips in order not to smile. Both groups rated how funny the cartoons were. The group that was not allowed to smile consistently rated the cartoons less funny than those who could view them and smile. Despite the hardwired experiences taking place, people were unable to have the chemical experience required to produce the level of emotion that they were consciously aware of. Studies like these show that facial expressions can give insight into an individual's internal mood. That is why mimicking another's facial expression elicits empathy (Bernstein et al. 2000). We also have learned that changing facial expression can actually alter our mood by changing our chemical experience (Davis and Palladino 2002). Many people have had the experience of being upset or angry and having something transpire that makes them laugh or smile. Immediately after the chemicals related to laughter are experienced, we realize that we cannot return to the same level of anger we previously were feeling.

Students who struggle in language acquisition or even second-language learners have been found to benefit from having facially expressive teachers. That is because the brain uses facial expressions to help bring meaning to language. It is even known that language acquisition is lowered when it is accomplished through tapes and videos because the human brain values communication more when it is provided by an individual over a machine. The study by McAuliffe found that children naturally focus on the human face in order to learn and understand. Children were far less able to focus on the same message when it was delivered by a tape than when it was spoken by a person (McAuliffe 2007, pp. 6–8). The teaching of how to read facial expressions appropriately is a vital role of mentors working with students who constantly misread social situations. These students can learn what expressions mean and how to respond better in order to lower negative reactions that they commonly experience. In addition, teachers and school administrators should be cautious not to become too emotional when handling a crisis situation. Since the amygdala is always screening, it will notice and is sensitive to the emotions of others. Emotionally charged responses will only increase the level of arousal and impulsive behaviors.

The amygdala seizes control of the hands more quickly and more directly than any other part of the human body. The amygdala constantly monitors hand movements to interpret internal moods such as anger or anxiety. Hand movements were man's earliest form of language because the amygdala could interpret and give hand gestures meaning (Allison et al. 2000, pp. 267–278). It is still believed that the gestures made by the hands are subconsciously monitored by the amygdala while one speaks. As a result, the amygdala subconsciously looks for compatibility between what is said and what is gestured. Neurological findings on individuals with communication disorders demonstrate a fundamental connection between speech and gestures. Brain damage that leads to the loss of mobility in limbs can compromise verbal communication. Patients with aphasia – who do not have the ability to speak or to understand speech – also find it difficult to gesture or understand signs made by others (Wachsmuth 2006). Many politicians receive coaching on hand-gesture cues that the amygdala interprets to mean truth. The politicians are then trained to consistently utilize these hand movements when speaking in public. Teachers and administrators should be aware that their hand movements are subconsciously being monitored at all times by students in order to determine believability.

Goldin-Meadow and colleagues published a study in the Journal of Educational Psychology showing that students in small math tutorials were more likely to learn new concepts when teachers used gestures that appropriately reinforced their message (Latta 2000). The teachers' gestures served not just to direct the students' attention to the numbers in the problem but conveyed problem-solving strategies not directly expressed in speech. Children were significantly less likely to learn if the teacher did not gesture or inadvertently used a gesture that did not correspond with her verbal instructions. Hand gestures are still important in language acquisition and processing even at this stage of man's language evolution. In 1998, a study published in Nature, Goldin-Meadow and Indiana University researcher Jana Iverson showed that children and adolescents who had been blind since birth spontaneously gesture when they are speaking, even if they know that they are speaking to another blind person. This speaks to the hardwired nature of gestures and helps explains why babies whose mothers utilize hand gestures while talking have been found to acquire words at a faster rate.

Awareness and utilization of the knowledge of the role hand gestures play in the expression of emotion and in aiding language can improve behavior management and academic instruction.

The amygdala also registers body movements and body posture. Many dramatic body movements are produced by the amygdala in response to stimuli interpreted as arousing. That is why dramatic movements made in front of someone in crisis increase his or her anxiety level. When a body movement is sustained for two seconds or more, it is then considered to be a posture. A posture is significant because it indicates a chemical secretion pattern high enough to maintain a position. Thus, mimicking someone's body posture can provide insight into his or her emotional condition because the mimicry will result in the slow secretion of the same chemical configuration found in the subject being mimicked. Recent research suggests that advanced emotional skills such as empathy are a result of the brain's ability to mirror external postures and gestures and have them automatically correlated to the chemical experience (Pellegrino et al. 1992, pp. 176–180; Rizzolatti and Arbib 1998, pp. 188–194). It is Mehrabian's research that discovered that about 55 percent of meaning in every interaction comes through nonverbal expression: gestures, postures, facial expressions, etc. It is behavior other than spoken or written communication that creates or represents a majority of the meaning.

Mimicking a person's body posture can also help establish rapport. It is important to note that the amygdala is aroused by differences. That arousal occurs because differences alert the survival system to be on guard. While in an alerted state, we are more likely to perceive things that are unfamiliar as threatening. Man's long-term history of perceiving different groups as threatening has been well chronicled. Stressful environments will crystallize the amygdala's constant level of arousal, producing impulsive behaviors often leading to impetuous acts and then to retaliation. If this level of arousal remains constant, the conflicts between groups will become persistent because the characteristics of the group alone will become enough to trigger the amygdala. It is important to remember that schools, due to the charge of having to provide everyone with free appropriate public education (FAPE), are mandated to enroll whoever comes regardless of culture or background. Once conflicts between groups reach an emotional level, the cortex will not be involved, and the differences associated with a certain group will alert the amygdala. This can result in irrational beliefs that will become an ever-present source of stimulation during times of stress.

When it comes to improving behaviors and social skills, schools should focus whenever possible on teaching concrete skills that can be learned and practiced over concepts alone. Concrete skills force the brain to change just by learning the behavior. When a new behavior is successfully attempted and receives a positive response, it will naturally reinforce the practice. Students easily can be taught the art of mimicking body posture in order to improve rapport. This is a nonthreatening method for teaching an important social skill. The act of mimicking a person's body posture places the focus on the other person and teaches the individual to notice signs that indicate when the person is feeling comfortable. This skill will begin to establish a good foundation for increased awareness, reading others, and responding accordingly.

Schools can reduce the occurrence of bullying behavior by teaching students who lack self-esteem and confidence to change their posture. Certain posture positions communicate to aggressive individuals that a person is a safe target. Schools can simply offer etiquette courses. Etiquette courses address rules for social encounters, grooming, dress, posture, appropriate greeting, eating habits, etc. Many of these rules are a natural outgrowth of a very formal attempt to appease the amygdala. An etiquette course provides an easy way to get all students to become aware of the universal rules that calm the amygdala. Knowing these rules will help students know what to do in many different social settings that they will face in the future.

Self-touch is another external expression of the internal condition. Self-touch reflects the arousal level of the sympathetic nervous system (Ekman and Friesen 1969, pp. 49–98; McGrew 1972, p. 268). Many view some self-touch behaviors as a method of self-medication. If chemical transference in the brain is required to produce any movement, then it stands to reason that repetitive actions can be a form of self-medication. The movement produces some chemical configuration that is appeasing and therefore is used to manage anxiety. However, the fact that these types of external self-medication patterns are often recognized by the amygdala can place one at risk. Teachers that learn to identify self-touch patterns become more skilled at intervening before a student has reached a level of chemical crisis. In addition, helping students to be more aware of the self-touch behaviors they engage in when becoming anxious can help them better monitor their behavior. This is important because these repetitive movement patterns subconsciously arouse predatory behaviors in certain individuals.

A study of sexual predators who randomly selected strangers as victims revealed that they intuitively looked for discrete self-touch behaviors and certain postures in identifying potential victims. Recent research indicates that although psychopaths lack the ability to read social cues and feel empathy, they possess a highly attuned ability to identify the nonverbal distress cues displayed by a victim (Blair et al. 2001, pp. 799–811). Self-touch also seems to be intricately involved in sexual arousal and in mating rituals. These primitive patterns of self-touch are as old as mankind itself. They are rooted in the drive to survive and self-perpetuate. Some dating services today teach insecure individuals how to read the occurrence of self-touch when on a date in order to improve their social skills and confidence.

Educators must be aware that spoken language is always accompanied by the automated nonverbal system. One's ability to manage this nonverbal system will determine if the amygdala will become calmed or alerted. In addition, students are constantly giving nonverbal signals of what they are experiencing internally. Our emphasis on the spoken word has created a level of insensitivity and lack of alertness. It is not surprising that it is only after a crisis when many individuals analyze nonverbal behaviors and recognize that there were indications of a problem. Educators also must learn to become extremely aware of their own state of arousal and the nonverbal signals they send out during those time periods. In addition, educators must constantly monitor for the nonverbal cues students exhibit in order to be more proactive in their behavior management.

Calibration is a proven method that teachers can learn in order to be aware of the physical movements identified in this chapter. Calibration is a method used to train individuals to become more aware of the brain's capacity to identify subconscious movement patterns. Teachers can be trained to calibrate an entire classroom while teaching. The process, when done correctly, does not require primary focus and therefore will not interfere with instruction. Teachers need only to learn the nonverbal movements to be alerted to, practice noticing them when in social settings within the community, and then they will notice that they will be more able to identify the behaviors when they occur in the classroom. Calibration exercises instruct people practicing the technique to look about four to six inches beside a person's ear and attempt to notice certain movements correlated to an emotion when they occur. An artificial method to induce an emotional reaction is to have the person you are calibrating approach you slowly. When the person's approach is within their comfort zone, their body will produce some involuntary movement associated with their feeling of discomfort. Once teachers become more sensitive in detecting these types of reactions, then they can attempt to scan people in larger social gatherings and see if they begin to detect the cues produced by the amygdala. Teachers should look for all the nonverbal cues identified in this chapter.

Over time, the amygdala has developed a second level of focus not concerned primarily with man. Through the evolution of the brain, the amygdala began to expand its focus to include tones, symbols, size, and environments. Although the focus on tones began with man, it later evolved to become one of the most sophisticated systems. The amygdala focuses on any tones that denote pain or danger (Givens 2005). This is why man has a hard time ignoring screams for help or a baby's cry. In addition, tones are a body function that the amygdala seizes control of in times of fear and anger. The amygdala increases the rate and the pitch of speech in times of arousal.

Man's natural association to tone is rooted in fetal development. The fetus becomes highly attuned to the mother's heartbeat (1962, pp. 753-763). Since a cord that secretes cortisol goes directly across the womb, whenever the infant is negatively impacted by this stress hormone, the mother's heartbeat will elevate. Many anthropologists believe that this is the reason man utilized drums prior to the inception of language to communicate strong emotions such as fear, danger, and celebration. Man would be able to tap out rhythms on drums that mimic heart rhythmic patterns that carried intuitive messages. Tones impact heart and blood rate; however, tones also impact the chemical balance in the brain.

Tone is an important aspect of teaching. Students all possess preferred tones that attack their focus. Therefore, teachers should seek to cover a wide range of tones throughout a lesson. Good teaching recommends the use of inflections, but the brain demands it. In addition, teachers must be aware that their tonality during a crisis will speak directly to the amygdala regardless of what is being said. Recent research indicates that tone of voice is actually processed differently in the brain and impacts emotional meaning (Scherer 1986, pp.143–65; Johnstone and Scherer 1999, pp. 2029-2032). The old adage "It's not what you say, but how you say it" is neurobiologically accurate.

The amygdala's focus on symbols is rooted in man's natural inclination to possess objects determined to be of value (Rizzolatti et al. 2006). Anthropologists have theorized that man's first objects were tools. Man utilized minerals and the natural resources available to do a task and determined some minerals and natural resources to be more appropriate for a job than others. This realization began to forge a pathway between an object's possessing emotional value in the amygdala and being reinforced in the nucleus accumbens. Once a mineral or natural object became useful in performing a task, such as hammering or cutting, man sought to possess more of it. Some anthropologists believe that labeling, the need to name an object of value, might be the root of formalized language. Since the pathway connecting an emotional attachment to an object is millions of years old, it is easy to understand why the reward pathway can be activated by simply seeing an object that has become important to an individual.

Brain science also has determined that an object could be replaced by a symbol or gesture and still trigger emotional attachment and reward. Many studies have viewed this phenomenon at work through brain resonance science. Individuals would be allowed to engage in a process during which they would see a symbol representing money and perform a physical task within an allotted time in order to be rewarded monetarily. Brain resonance pictures indicated that this symbol triggered the hippocampus and the prefrontal cortex processing the visual image. Then the amygdala would be active in a manner indicating emotional value. Once the pattern was established and repeated, the reward pathway would be activated. If the pattern persisted, the prefrontal cortex would presecrete a form of dopamine, indicating that the reward pathway was going to be activated. This is the same process observed by individuals suffering from a substance addiction. Referred to in the chapter on climate, heroin addicts who utilize a spoon to prepare the drug will eventually only have to see the spoon in order to secrete dopamine in the prefrontal cortex. The secretion of dopamine in the prefrontal cortex is responsible for motivating action. This is why associating symbols to identified practices is a crucial step. That means the desire or craving for the behavior will follow. It is this motivation that explains why all habitual behaviors are rewarded in the brain.

Advertisers adhere to this science and apply it well. They create a symbol and associate it with an emotion. Once the person engages in the process a few times and it is reinforced in the brain, it will become a practice that can become habitual. This is why advertisers utilize commercials that are played over and over. Repetition is a proven method of activating the reward pathway. If a behavior exists, it can be triggered by the commercial. This process explains why an individual can be watching television and see a food commercial come on and be motivated to get something to eat. Eating is an action that is already reinforced in the brain; if the correct trigger is seen, the action can be motivated. Once the reward pathway is activated, a practice will become habitual. This illustrates why it is so important to associate symbols with desired practices in education. It is important to remember that since a symbol is recognized by the amygdala, it is a part of the response process even in times of stress.

Schools should seek to apply the same science when they are attempting to establish a new value of behavioral practice. The association of the value or practice with a symbol is a necessary element in the brain motivating the practice. Once the symbol comes to represent the value or practice, it should be prominently displayed so that it becomes an additional source of motivation. Schools need to focus on this element of the science since the complaint of not knowing how to motivate students is so widely heard.

The amygdala's focus on size is also a result of an innate response called looming (Givens 1986, pp. 145–167). The looming phenomenon is actually the result of a self-preservation response. At about fourteen days of age, a baby automatically avoids objects that increase in size too quickly, causing rapid iris dilation. This response is designed to help humans be alerted to rapidly approaching objects in order to avoid them. The innate association of fear to rapidly increasing size explains man's belief that constructing large structures symbolizes power. Although building things larger is a very effective way for empires to communicate threat and power to other nations, it is not a good model for education.

Larger settings increase stimuli, which increases anxiety and results in lowering the ability to learn and raising the occurrence of impulsive behaviors. Schools should seek to lower anxiety through measures that reduce stimuli. Schools can stagger class transitions in order to reduce movement and noise in the hallways. Classrooms can utilize learning centers in order for students to work in smaller groups. Students with special needs should be placed in smaller settings with a lower student-to-teacher ratio. In certain cases in which the student is at high risk and he or she struggles with a certain academic subject, scheduled times for one-on-one instruction might be required.

Dr. James Garbarino, director of the Center for the Human Rights of Children at Loyola University Chicago, states that one of the most significant impacts on education was the shift after the 1950s to let school size exceed five hundred students. He claims that the increase in school size impacted the marginal students who would have been permitted and even encouraged to participate in a smaller school setting. This prevented many students from being allowed to build and develop assets that would have been essential to life success in the future. In addition, in the smaller school setting, teachers know each student on a more interpersonal level. This prevents students from falling through the cracks and feeling invisible. A common refrain heard after many a school tragedy is "I wish I had just paid a little more attention to that student."

The issue of size provides a perfect example of the way environments impact the amygdala. Man is designed to adjust to environments that are consistent, predictable, and safe. This process is called habituation. Environmental structures and routines will lower the arousal response of the amygdala with consistent exposure. The problem is that children suffering from emotional or physical disorders usually take a longer time to adapt to change. Climates can facilitate the transitions of at-risk individuals by ritualizing them, thus reducing many negative behaviors. Homes that ritualize all the major transitions of the day are the most successful in addressing the range of issues children face. Once again, the message is clear. School environments should structure admission, lunch, dismissal, and all other major transitions in the day in order to prevent behavioral problems and increase academic performance. Remember, transition rituals must be specifically designed and reinforced in a manner that allows students to interpret each action as positive and safe.

CHAPTER II

Isopraxism

We must become the change we want to see.

– Gandhi

Since the human brain focuses on the nonverbal cues of others, it is only logical that this level of monitoring impacts man's behavior. The constant monitoring can profoundly influence behavioral practices in certain situations. Educators should never forget that their behavior is constantly teaching. When modeled behavior influences the behavior of another, it is called *isopraxism.*

Isopraxism is the term used to explain the scientific phenomenon of why human behavior is subconsciously influenced by social bonding, attraction, consistently modeled behaviors, and behaviors experienced in trauma (Harris 2003, pp. 525–31). The amygdala is prewired to focus on human behavior; this means that what humans do is always registered in the brain. There are three laws of isopraxism:

- That which is modeled the most during childhood and adolescent development is predictive of how the individual will behave as an adult.
- That which is modeled during times of extreme emotion will be emulated dependent on the individual's level of emotional health and perceived stress.
- That which is modeled and found attractive will be mimicked.

That which is modeled the most during child and adolescent development is predictive of how the individual will behave as an adult.

A good example of the first law of isopraxism is the profound impact of the initial behavioral model of a child. The infant's amygdala is programmed to read the primary caretaker's behaviors. These behaviors become the initial model of social practices. More importantly, the primary caretaker's behavioral patterns are the model during key developmental stages and, eventually, during times of emotion and crisis. This is the reason why children grow up to parent as their parents did. Parental responses in crisis or emotional situations are stored in the amygdala. Thus, when adults encounter their first emotionally charged discipline issue, they find themselves behaving like their parents. It is because the responses of their parents were modeled consistently, and/or were emotionally significant. The responses of our parents live in the amygdala, and similar emotional experiences with our own children trigger these memories, influencing our behavior.

Teaching practices, like parenting practices, are modeled during this stage of development. Students are exposed to a consistent range of teaching practices beginning at preschool and continuing throughout college. This is why teachers mimic the models of past instructors even if they did not particularly approve of them. Teaching practices, like parenting styles, are difficult to alter. They are based on the dominant model that was present for over seventeen years prior to a teacher's ever providing a day of instruction in her own classroom. That is why mentoring might be the most effective method for teaching new effective instructional practices. Teachers need to see it done, practice it with others, and then solo the methods while having support and feedback.

The science of isopraxism also begins to explain why pervasive models are so powerful. It is common knowledge that the greatest predictor of whether a child will maintain consistent employment in adulthood is whether the parent(s) model going to work on a consistent daily basis. That is because the models engage in the behavior so consistently that it becomes an expected behavior. It is only logical that other pervasive practices existing within a home become the model for the future. Children exposed to healthy marriages are better able to emulate those behaviors later in their own lives. On the other hand, those exposed to dysfunctional marriages are at risk for duplicating those negative practices when under stress.

It is also likely that when a practice is modeled in the home and in the community, it will increase the likelihood of emulation. For example, resiliency studies that looked at risk factors prevalent in a community, such as teen pregnancy, found that attitudes within the community were likely to tolerate and even justify the behavior. In cases where pervasive behaviors exist within the home and also in the community, it is likely that the behavioral pattern would be even more prevalent.

The mystical concept of personal attraction is in many ways demystified by the laws of isopraxism. Attraction can be defined as preferences, conscious or subconscious, developed because of the influences of behavioral patterns that are either persistent or modeled in times of development or extreme emotion. These experiences are stored in the amygdala and are available when one is emotional and likely to be impulsive.

This begins to explain some forms of attraction and mimicking behaviors. On one end of the spectrum, man is exposed to a very healthy adult model. These positive, strong memories are stored in the amygdala. Over time, these memories influence what is thought when a similar stimulus is encountered. That is why people often marry other people who possess characteristics similar to those of their parent(s). However, this also explains the other end of the attraction spectrum. Individuals exposed to negative models that induce severe trauma also have these negative examples available in the amygdala during emotional times. It is important to remember that all persistent, highly sensory emotional experiences can be reinforced in the brain. What is reinforced is likely to become a persistent behavioral pattern. The brain does not make moral judgments on what it reinforces. This process provides a rational explanation as to why many traumatic behaviors that are cognitively recognized as bad are often reproduced by those exposed to similar behaviors.

That which is modeled during times of extreme emotion will be emulated by certain temperaments when under stress.

The amygdala retains memories that are highly emotional, meaning that both the best and worst experiences are remembered. It is important to remember that since memories in the amygdala are seldom comprehensive, it is easier for the amygdala to record the chemical response pattern while suppressing the related stimuli. This means that a behavior can be triggered by a past trauma in which there is no conscious memory but in which the amygdala response pattern is still released. That is why the second law of isopraxism states that experiences that produce extreme emotion can produce the same behaviors in certain individuals. This begins to explain how someone can be abused, cognitively hate the experience and yet, when experiencing stress, abuse someone else. This finding might help individuals to understand the cycle of sexual abuse. It seems that individuals who possess a more difficult temperament and suffer from significant chemical imbalance are at higher risk of duplicating extreme behaviors that they have experienced when they are under stress. Individuals with more shy and anxious temperaments are more prone to have extreme actions done to them experienced again. This begins to explain a significant feature of the perpetual victim. Cognitive therapies performed with these profiled aggressors and victims seem to fail. This is because their cognitive understanding is unable to help them when they are experiencing stress. Their past experiences related to the victimization was so traumatic that it produces enough arousal to prevent the cortex from mediating against the impulsivity of the amygdala.

That which is modeled and found attractive will be mimicked.

Children are more likely to mimic new behaviors that are modeled by adults whom they like and respect. This is why close friends seem to take on behaviors of the other that they find attractive. It is not unusual for very close friends to begin to speak, dress, and even demonstrate similar mannerisms.

Isopraxism demands that the adults at school practice what they preach, model new behaviors, and consistently maintain the behavior over time. Every ritual developed to improve the educational climate must be modeled by the adults first. The change of adult behavior first is the key to the success of most educational initiatives. This means that programmatic success in educational settings should focus on adult and not student behavior. It is impossible for a student suffering from severe chemical imbalance to reconcile why the adults in a school consistently violate a rule they want students to model. For example, if students are expected to walk on the right-hand side of the hallway, it is imperative that the adults adhere to the same rule. The students most at risk are always monitoring human behavior because they tend to be more anxious, and as a result, their amygdalae are more active. Not only they will tend to notice behavioral inconsistencies of the adults, but also they will be less able to ignore the inconsistency and still adhere to the rule.

It is important to remember that every validated strategy ultimately is crafted by human hands. There are no strategies that negate human behavior. Ultimately, the success of any educational program is related to the behaviors of those responsible for carrying it out. Therefore, there is no perfect program that will address presenting issues; there are superior methods of implementation that are focused on increasing the consistency of adult behavior. This is why schools must master how to design practices so that they will be reinforced in the human brain. It is reinforcement in the brain that is the key to developing persistent practice.

CHAPTER 12

The Reward Pathway

The highest reward for a person's toil is not what they get for it, but what they become by it.

– John Ruskin

R*eward* is such a highly used term in the field of education that it needs to be defined in order to avoid existing misconceptions. The definition of *reward*, when used in the context of the brain, is *that which is learned in a sensory manner and arouses positive feeling in the amygdala, resulting in dopamine shifts in the reward pathway, making the action highly desired.* The reward pathway or the *nucleus accumbens* was first discovered as a region of the brain that was activated when humans engaged in repetitive behaviors associated with survival: eating, drinking, and sex. Scientists noticed that when humans engaged in these practices, the region of the brain known as the *nucleus accumbens* would activate dopamine during the behavior (Lowinson et al. 1997). Later, studies of individuals who suffered from eating disorders or possessed no sexual drive revealed that the nucleus accumbens was no longer secreting the same levels of dopamine when they engaged in these behaviors. Researchers concluded that the reward pathway is the source of habitual behavior. It is activated when people engage in practices they find rewarding. When there is no activation in this region, the motivation for even innate behaviors will dissipate and even cease.

Later studies on the nucleus accumbens found that this same region of the brain is also involved in substance addictions (Chiara et al. 1999, pp. 461–85). It is now known that many chemical substances abused by man mimic dopamine in the reward pathway when they enter the human body. This means that the behavior automatically mimics the reward process, and that accounts for the behavior becoming addictive. The original theory was that certain substances, if taken, would be addictive. However, this finding was not consistent among all individuals who experimented with substances. Additional research discovered that certain individuals are more susceptible to becoming addicted than others.

It seems that individuals who are susceptible to becoming addicted are those who share a deficiency in the dopamine D2 receptor (Blum et al. 1996). This receptor is involved in providing reward in the nucleus accumbens. The inability of dopamine D2 receptors to be activated by certain prewired activities creates a vacuum of dopamine D2 in the brain. A deficiency of dopamine D2 receptors causes an inability to feel reward and achieve chemical balance in the brain: the chemical equivalent to normalcy. Therefore, once any action triggers dopamine D2 or something the brain perceives to be dopamine, a strong desire to repeat the behavior in order for the brain to feel this sense of balance is created. Individuals with healthy brain functions produce enough dopamine D2 daily.

Even many daily practices are enabled by dopamine reinforcement. Man is able to experience chemical benefit from all behaviors he trains himself to repeat: no matter how mundane or inconsequential. When a healthy person's brain perceives it is receiving dopamine D2 from a new source, it does not respond with the same craving to repeat the behavior because the brain gets sufficient levels of dopamine daily. As a result, individuals with healthy reward pathways do not experience the same physical response when abusing a substance. However, for individuals who do not produce dopamine D2, substance use will immediately make the brain feel better than it has during their day-to-day existence.

Addictions for individuals who have deficient dopamine D2 receptors will intensify over time because the brain adapts quickly. The brain administers natural chemicals in a very precise manner. When a substance is abused, overwhelming amounts enter the brain all at once. The brain perceives this to be a result of an overproduction of dopamine. If high levels of dopamine become a common occurrence, the brain will make adjustments by reducing the natural production of dopamine. This will lower the natural production of dopamine by individuals who do not produce normal amounts of this brain chemical. After a short period of time, they will become dependent on external substances for most of their dopamine reinforcement. This is the scientific explanation as to why most substance abusers find that the initial feelings experienced when first taking the substance wane over time, and they are forced to abuse greater quantities in order to achieve the initial feelings of euphoria. Over time, the feeling of euphoria will fade, and the abuse will take on a role of maintenance in order to avoid low physiological levels: this experience is better known as withdrawal.

It is important to note that the reward pathway is also involved with eating, sleeping, and feelings of depression. Infants who struggle to adapt to the environment or to be soothed by their primary caretaker often demonstrate poor eating and sleeping patterns. This is a very early sign of an abnormally functioning reward pathway. This is why altered eating and sleeping patterns are indicators of emotional disorders. Effective treatment must first seek to stabilize sleeping and eating patterns in order to improve the chemical balance of the brain. Individuals who suffer from altered eating and sleeping patterns usually require regimented environments to function better. This offers further support for why it is so important for schools to create predictable structures that promote positive feelings of reward.

Current research has indicated that a deficiency in the dopamine D2 receptors related to the reward pathway is the root cause of most emotional disorders (Cloninger 1983, pp. 487–96; Blum et al. 1996 pp. 396-400). Researchers have coined this problem reward deficiency syndrome (RDS). RDS is the inability to experience reward from ordinary everyday activities. The ability of the brain to produce dopamine during persistent daily activities produces a feeling of well-being. The disruption of this system produces anxiety, anger, and other bad feelings. That is why reduction of anxiety is so important for successful educational programming. It is also why creating rituals that are aligned to positive feelings that are rewarding is so crucial for establishing productive educational environments.

Another important finding is that individuals who suffer from RDS are susceptible to addictions to pain. Pain triggers the reward pathway because it activates chemicals released to administer pain relief (Gear et al. 1999, pp. 7175–81; Horvitz 2000, pp. 651–56; Zubieta et al. 2003, pp.1240–43). This is done by releasing both opioids and dopamine. By activating the nucleus accumbens, pain itself becomes a rewarding experience. This is not a cognitive process. Individuals with RDS do not usually engage in actions that produce pain and confuse it with feelings of reward. Subconsciously, the activation of the reward pathway produces a drive to repeat the activation of the reward pathway. The brain does not make moral judgments on behaviors; rather, it seeks to establish chemical balance. If an individual has a normally functioning reward pathway, the activation of pain relief in the nucleus accumbens is not as rewarding as the dopamine released through daily activities. Therefore, they experience little motivation to engage in behaviors that result in pain to feel rewarded. This begins to explain why individuals with RDS will have difficulty ending negative behavioral patterns, leaving abusive situations, or stopping the use of substances. The negative behavior is the most reinforcing practice they have established. Until other more positive practices are established and rewarded, the chemical motivation to stop is absent. Schools must therefore understand that habitual negative behaviors, such as chronic bullying, are similar to addictions and cannot easily be extinguished.

The reward pathway does not function independently. Understanding how the reward pathway works can help educators design more productive interventions. The reward pathway seems to be interrelated to the prefrontal cortex, especially the magnocellular (orbitofrontal cortex) section of the prefrontal cortex. The magnocellular section receives input from the ventral or object-processing visual stream, which focuses on smell, sight, taste, touch, and movement. It plays a crucial roll in the development of goal-directed motivation (Damasio 1994; Rolls 1996, pp. 1433–44). Goal-directed motivation has to do with the ability of a person to make a cognitive decision and be motivated to carry it out. It is this association to motivation that has led researchers to discover that the orbitofrontal cortex has a role in the processing of reward information (Iversen and Mishkin 1970, pp. 376–86; Dias et al. 1996, pp. 69–72). Researchers concluded that the orbitofrontal cortex responds to emotions of reward or aversion produced by the amygdala. Its correlation to the hippocampus is logical. It focuses on many of the same sensory inputs as the hippocampus, with the exception of auditory processing.

It is the orbitofrontal cortex that is able to associate a sensory trigger to reward. Once a sensory cue is associated to the experience of reward, through the repeated activation of the reward pathway, the orbitofrontal cortex will forge the association and begin to secrete dopamine (Volkow and Fowler 2000, pp. 318–25; Schultz et al. 2000, pp. 272–84). Researchers conditioned a rat to eat cocaine from a spoon. Each time the rat ate the cocaine from the spoon, the researchers gave the rat manual stimulation in the reward pathway. After some conditioning, the scientist found that VTA dopamine receptors found in the orbitofrontal cortex would secrete dopamine at the sight of the spoon, intensifying the motivation to engage in the behavior in order to activate the reward pathway.

The amygdala and the hippocampus are also intricately involved in the reward pathway. The emotional response of the amygdala to a stimulus seems to determine if the orbitofrontal cortex will make a positive association between stimulus and reward. Since the orbitofrontal cortex does not process auditory data, but sensory data, it is dependent on the input of the sensory data process passed on by the hippocampus. The hippocampus passes on sensory data at the same time that the amygdala is relaying emotional data.

The development of a persistent behavior is dependant on the new behavior stimulating all the aspects of the reward pathway. First, the behavior being taught must be sensory in nature. Without some sensory processing being incorporated in the ritual, there will be no sensory information to be processed by the orbitofrontal cortex in order to provide motivation.

The next step is to align positive emotions with the sensory behavioral process being taught. Each individual has a set of values that successfully reinforces him or her. However, behavioral science has taught that identifying what those values are for each individual can be difficult. The process can be expedited by aligning the sensory behavioral process to one of the three universal perceptions that humans have innately: need to feel safe, need to feel wanted, and the need to feel successful. Whenever a behavior is being taught, it is important to remember that the law of isopraxism demands that the behavior be modeled consistently by those teaching the behavior. This will expedite learning and motivation in the amygdala.

Once a sensory behavioral practice is successfully associated with a positive emotion in the amygdala, the reward pathway over time will become activated. That is because the reinforcement for the emotion is already established, and the nucleus accumbens can be consistently activated by predictable, persistent practices. The process of periodic external reinforcement has been proven to further enhance the reward process. This can be accomplished by periodic external reinforcement. There seem to be two forms of external reinforcement that influence the reward pathway: unexpected reinforcement or periodic reinforcement that builds anticipation.

Once the reward pathway is consistently activated by the behavior, a sensory trigger can be associated to further increase motivation. The association of a symbol to trigger the activation of VTA dopamine in the orbitofrontal cortex will further improve the rate of adherence to the new behavior. The science clearly illustrates that a new behavior must be taught through a specific sensory process. The behavior then must be associated with a positive emotion that is maintained long enough to become rewarding.

Schools can design new behavioral responses to replace existing patterns. However, this type of intervention will require targeted strategies that will be consistently practiced and reinforced. Therefore, effective behavioral interventions are not only the ability to follow the science in designing the strategy but also the discipline to maintain the practice long enough for the brain to begin to reinforce the new behavior. This, once again, places the emphasis on consistent human behavior.

CHAPTER 13

A Resiliency-Based Understanding of Children and Adolescents

The frightening thing about heredity and environment
is that parents provide both.

– Walt Schreibman

The issue of educating the high-risk child baffles educators and treatment providers alike. The problem begins at the initial point of assessment and identification. The battery of assessments conducted mainly identifies emotional and cognitive deficits. Educators complain that the assessment process determines classifications of exceptionality and placement rather than explaining how to better educate the exceptional student. This means special education is placing emphasis on identification of deficits rather than on incorporating successful strategies that will improve outcomes with high-risk students. It is evident that this approach has had long-term systems implications in the field of education. The assessment process is more closely aligned with budget allocation than with insightful discovery, which would lead to improved student performance. Also, teacher-training programs devote a great deal of time to helping future educators identify disabilities while having dropped pedagogy from the curriculum. The focus on assessing disability is so pervasive that interagency collaboration efforts between child service agencies are often thwarted by conflicting information based on evaluations conducted by each agency in its narrow discipline. As a result, it is difficult for agencies to agree on client profile, much less a uniform course of action. One might be forced to conclude that any approach that focuses primarily on the identification of pathology rather than methods for improving outcomes is flawed due to its failure to prioritize solutions.

Resiliency theory, on the other hand, is providing some answers for better assessing and educating the high-risk student. Resiliency theory seeks to determine why certain at-risk individuals experience success in the face of seemingly insurmountable odds in life. Resiliency studies identify specific risk factors that have placed individuals at greater risk for failure, as well as specific protective factors that seem to insulate certain at-risk individuals from experiencing poor outcomes in life (Werner 1989, pp. 72–81). By incorporating resiliency theory into assessment design, one is ensured of evaluating both a wide range of disabilities and risk factors and the existing strengths and specific interventions that should improve outcomes. A resiliency-based assessment approach provides a method for conducting a true biopsychosocial assessment that is not disability-based, not narrow in its focus, and is outcome driven. Adopting such an approach can provide an opportunity to rethink the assessment process and functional assessments and the administration of budgetary allocations. Also, a resiliency-based approach could return the emphasis of special education training and interagency collaboration back to effective planning and improved outcome.

The Identification of Specific Risk Factors Associated to Poor Life Outcomes

Resiliency theory provides individuals with a paradigm that is not disability based and that merges assessment with treatment planning. This assessment approach is based on a number of longitudinal studies of large groups of children growing up in community settings (Garmezy et al. 1984; Rae-Grant et al. 1988; Rutter 1985; Werner and Smith 1982; Wyman et al. 1991). Within these groups of children, many characteristics of the children and their families were examined, and the life course of the child was charted into adulthood. These large studies contained hundreds of children with outcomes varying from successful to abysmal. In looking at the characteristics of children with difficult outcomes, the researchers have identified consistent *risk factors*, which are often associated with the development of negative outcomes, such as school failure, psychiatric illness, criminal involvement, vocational instability, and poor social relationships later in life (Vance and Sanchez 1994). The risk factors that have been repeatedly identified are listed below.

A. In the Child

- Fetal drug/alcohol effects
- Premature birth or complications
- Difficult temperament
- Shy temperament
- Neurological impairment
- Low IQ < 80
- Chronic medical disorder

- Psychiatric disorder
- Repeated aggression
- Substance abuse
- Delinquency
- Academic failure

B. Family Characteristics

- Low socioeconomic status
- Large family with four or more children
- Siblings born within two years of child
- Parent with emotional disorder
- Parent with substance abuse
- Parent with criminality

C. Family/Experiential

- Poor infant attachment to mother
- Long-term absence of caregiver in infancy
- Witness to extreme conflict or violence
- Neglect
- Separation/divorce/single parent
- Negative parent-child relationship
- Sexual abuse
- Physical abuse
- Removal from home
- Frequent family moves
- Teen pregnancy

The Impact of Protective Factors on Mitigating Risk and Improving Outcomes

Risk factors do not invariably lead to problems in the lives of children but rather increase the probability that such problems will arise. In studying a multicultural group of children in Hawaii, Werner (1982) found that if a child had three or more risk factors, the likelihood of later negative psychosocial outcomes was substantially increased. Interestingly, the studies show that which risk factors are present is less significant than how many. This suggests that when these risk factors accumulate in the life of a child, there is a tendency toward the range of negative outcomes, regardless of which specific risk factors are operative. It follows that the damaging effects of multiple risk factors apply across gender, race, culture, and disability categories. This conclusion has been supported by studies in a variety of socioeconomic and demographic populations (Vance and Sanchez 1994, pp. 1–2).

Many of these factors seem obvious and have been suspected for many years to lead to poor outcomes. For example, low socioeconomic status has been linked to poor psychosocial outcome. Likewise, substance abuse or specific psychiatric illnesses have well-studied natural histories and devastating effects. What is less obvious and has not been studied until recently, is that a certain number of children have successful outcomes in life despite having many of these risk factors. These survivors of risk have been labeled "resilient" children. In studying resilient children and their families, researchers have begun to identify important features that seem to confer protection against the poor outcomes usually associated with a life comprising many risk factors. These so-called protective factors confer protection regardless of the child's diagnosis, disability, or IQ. It has also been shown that the greater the number of risk factors, the greater the number of protective factors needed to promote a positive outcome. The specific protective factors identified in various studies are listed below.

A. Qualities of the Child

- Positive temperament, adaptable, "easy baby"
- Autonomy and independence as a toddler
- Problem-solving skills at school age
- Gets along with others
- Interpersonally engaging, "likable"
- Sense of humor
- Empathy
- Perceived competencies
- IQ > 100
- Good reader
- Internal locus of control as a teenager
- High hopes and expectations for the future

B. Family Characteristics

- Lives at home
- Positive attachment with parents
- Perception of parental warmth
- Inductive, consistent discipline by parent
- Established routines in the home

C. Social Support from Outside the Family

- Adult mentor for child outside immediate family
- Extra adult help for caretaker of family
- Support for child from friends

- Support for child from school
- Support for family from church
- Support for family from workplace

In many ways, resiliency provides a blueprint for increasing capacity. It is the identification of protective factors that provide insight into what specific change can occur in an individual's life that can improve his/her opportunity for success. It is clear that each protective factor produces profound change in the human brain. These changes in the brain correlate with improved brain functioning. The improvement of brain functioning and the restoring of homeostasis have a rippling benefit on an individual's capacity. The logic is sound:

- Protective factors improve brain function.
- Improved brain function improves homeostasis.
- Improved homeostasis restores neurogenesis.
- Restored neurogenesis increases brain functioning and learning.
- Improved capacity to learn increases adaptability.
- Adaptability is an indicator of good mental health.

CHAPTER 14

Behavior Management

*The key to behavior management is the ability to promote
the perception of safety.*

– Horacio Sanchez

Behavior management begins at the level of prevention and preparation. Failure to implement preventive measures in the classroom will result in teachers reacting to a higher number of problems. Reacting to problems is not an effective management approach because emotions reduce the ability of the brain to think logically and instead trigger nonverbal behaviors that intuitively arouse others. In addition, when a teacher mismanages a crisis situation, it can undermine the concept of safety and security, therefore creating a level of chemical instability related to the class that will increase the occurrence of similar behaviors in the future. Simply stated, some early mistakes are difficult to undo.

The goal of behavior management is to meet the needs of the primitive brain – more specifically, the emotional processing system in the primitive brain called the amygdala. By soothing the beast within hardwired primitive response patterns, teachers can produce more thoughtful and emotionally stable students. Ultimately, the ability to meet the needs of the amygdala can best be achieved by creating a classroom paradigm designed to meet the most significant hardwired needs of the amygdala. The universal hardwired needs of the amygdala are three: the need to be safe, the need to feel wanted, and the need to be successful. When these needs are being met, man can maximize his learning and intellectual capacities.

Man is a biopsychosocial creature. His strongest biological drive is survival. That is why the need to feel safe is primary. His psychological needs are best described as the outcome of his biological and social existence. Along with the drive to survive, man is hardwired to be a social creature. Man's survival is initially dependent on caring relationships since he or she is unable to care for himself/herself at birth. His or her emotional condition is dependent on having predictable safe environments with significant loving relationships. The feelings of safety and love both play a large role in emotional stability. These two perceptions continue to play a significant role in man's ability to develop physically, emotionally, and cognitively. Therefore, when an educator structures a classroom, the initial emphasis should be to make students feel safe and wanted in order to maximize success. Failure to attend to these primitive needs will reduce academic achievement and increase behavioral issues. It is correct that many students have these needs met at home. However, these needs are part of an optimum productive learning environment. And for many students from less structured homes, school is where many of these needs are met.

The first thing a classroom must do is establish order. Remember, civilization brought predictability to daily existence, allowing man's amygdala to calm down and the cortex to be more readily engaged. This resulted in the growth of the cortex and the birth of reasonable man. The irony is that man incorporated an emotional reactive process to protect and maintain his emotional need for order. Social man formed clans. Clans met some primary needs of the amygdala: safety, socialization, and success. Clans were a collection of individuals who shared things in common, made rules to ensure safety, and worked collectively to be more successful. In order to protect this newfound order, man made rules. When established rules were violated, man felt order was jeopardized and reacted emotionally. This led to the establishment of harsh punishments that ranged from public ridicule to death.

This law and punishment system led to the need to develop institutions that could respond to those who repeatedly ignored the rules. The rise of the legal system is based on a primitive emotional desire to maintain order through extracting some emotional satisfaction. Man has and will continue to undertake drastic measures to eliminate emotions from the legal process to ensure fairness. This has proven to be a difficult task. That is why laws and the legal system maintain such detailed records, rules, and procedures. However, the premise is flawed at its initial assumption since man is an emotional creature when dealing with emotional issues. The meticulous records the legal system maintains have become a living testament that decision making can be irrational when emotions are high. Cases of gross injustice have been recorded whenever emotions could not be separated from the legal process. Emotional man has often brought irrational lawsuits against others, stemming from some arousing event. There have been many cases of gross injustice due to the emotions surrounding a crime that have led to the death sentence of innocent men. Ultimately, man's prime example of rehabilitation, the prison system, has always struggled to be anything more than inhumane treatment. In unsafe places where man feels unwanted and unsuccessful, the primitive drives of survival become paramount, and impulsivity becomes the norm.

Little attention was given to the occurrence that most laws grew out of universal needs held by the primitive brain. Most individuals not only desired these rules but also naturally adhered to them. Therefore, those who violate the rules must be either acting based on situational arousal or have something negatively impacting the brain's inherent system. Simply put, men who violate laws actually have the same primitive drive for survival so heightened that it hinders perceptions and ultimately leads to impulsive behaviors. In other words, these individuals actually need a greater sense of order to allow their amygdalae to feel safe. The existence of rules is not enough to bestow a feeling of safety to those who struggle with impulsivity. The fact that one is unable to maintain himself or herself can become a source of stress and something to be circumvented.

The concept that punishment will get these individuals to adhere to established laws is irrational since punishment will only lead to a greater perception of threat. Man reached this conclusion by observing the behavior of other healthy humans. The concept that man can obey all the laws governing human behavior was a conclusion reached by the success of the majority. This approach to all rules continues today. Where identified students are struggling behaviorally, a school or teacher implements rules to address the inappropriate practices of these students. Once the healthy students consistently meet the new objective, there is an expectation that everyone within the same time frame should have complied. This is a false assumption based on the premise that people who are inherently more capable became the standard for those who are inherently less capable. Most teachers would not expect someone with a brain injury that has impacted his memory to recall information at the same rate as a student with a healthy brain without limitations. Yet we view following rules completely differently.

Unfortunately, the increased threat of punishment will actually lead to increased impulsivity. The classroom must therefore be able to establish social order without increasing the amygdala's level of arousal and assume that all students will not be able to meet the expectations at the same time. A truism for those who suffer from the greatest chemical imbalance is that the fear of failure and the inability to meet expected behavioral norms lead to rebellious actions. So what is the answer?

The answer is teaching and motivating social practices rather than establishing stress-producing rules. This is not to say that educators should not have rules. Rules are necessary; however, equally important is the need to place emphasis on teaching the practices that will ensure that violations occur with less frequency. Classroom structure can be achieved by teaching the behaviors required for academic and behavioral success. Classroom "don't-do rules" are replaced with "desired practices." Since the basic, primitive needs of man are the same, students in a guided process will consistently produce the same basic rules needed to establish a safe environment.

Rules are less threatening when they are clearly requested by those who bear the burden of adhering to them. However, rules or desired practices are just a starting point and not the conclusion of establishing an orderly classroom.

The Process

This section does not attempt to outline the only method that can be used to establish social order, but it illustrates a proven approach to help those not familiar with the concept. This process will meet all the inherent rules required in the science to successfully structure a classroom.

Every teacher has to engage in an activity that helps students experience why an orderly classroom is more desirable than a chaotic one. Many teachers assume that all students understand how to behave appropriately and are motivated to do so. Such an assumption leads to teachers being surprised and unprepared when violations occur. Teachers should focus their initial attention on teaching the behaviors they want and creating an atmosphere in which students are motivated to adhere to desired classroom practices. This is best done by designing an experience that helps students associate inappropriate behaviors to the internal feelings that chaos produces and desired practices with the internal feeling of balance that the human brain desires.

Teachers need to teach through a carefully designed experience that allows students to sense what chaos and order feel like. This can be achieved by developing a teaching module designed to provide rich sensory experience of both extremes: sight, sounds, touch, smells associated with strong existing emotions. The goal is to establish a negative association with disorder and a positive one with order. This experience can be most effectively designed by utilizing two techniques: framing and anchoring.

Framing, according to many psychologists, linguists, and cognitive scientists, is a process used to facilitate the thinking process (Goffman 1974, p. 21; Nelson et al. 1997, pp. 221–46). It is a process used to invoke a particular image or idea and attach it to another. Examples of framing are all around us, from politics to television. The term liberal spending Democrats was used by the Republicans to frame the fiscal policies of their rivals. This association became so strong that many people failed to take note that in a Republican-controlled government, spending was often higher. Polls showed that the general public associated a free-spending approach to the Democrats. The framing process associated two separate concepts, liberal spending and Democrats. By constantly invoking a particular idea, the framing party was able to effectively control the discourse, thus setting the agenda. The goal is for teachers to frame classroom behaviors: that negative behaviors lead to an overwhelming feeling of chaos and that positive practices lead to a feeling of internal stability. It is important to note that if teachers fail to frame classroom behaviors, the students will do it for them. Whenever a student makes a negative comment related to a teacher directive that is perceived by the rest of the class as witty or funny, the student has effectively framed and anchored the action. Whenever the request is made, students will recall the association made by the student and recall the emotion of it's being funny.

Another technique teachers should utilize to structure their classrooms successfully is anchoring. Anchoring is the technique that is used to help the brain value what has been framed. This step allows something that has just been introduced to gain internal importance to the brain (Krugman 1985, pp. 526–30). Anchoring is a psychological term used to describe the brain's tendency to utilize emotional values when making decisions. During the normal decision-making process, individuals rely on related information and values to reach daily conclusions. It is emotional values that influence stronger behavioral patterns. Therefore, the decision-making process can be adjusted to consider new information if it is emotionally anchored to something positive. The key is to connect the information that is being anchored to an external trigger. A trigger can be a wide range of sensory cues associated with the emotional experience: verbal phrases, physical touches or sensations, certain sights and sounds, and internal dialogue, just to name a few. For example, when the student made the comment concerning the new behavior, and it resulted in laughter, the request was anchored to the emotion of silly or foolish. The phrase the student made becomes the external trigger. The student only has to repeat the phrase for everyone in the class to remember the emotion. The goal is to utilize this same technique and anchor negative behaviors to an overwhelming feeling of chaos and desired practices to internal calm. This will result in students actually having negative associations to inappropriate behaviors.

Once the classroom is framed and anchored, rules and desired practices are added. Although rules are important, they are not the focal point of this exercise. The brain-based approach requires that we adhere to certain guidelines when developing rules and desired practices.

- Rules and desired practices must be stated as specific actions.
- Each rule or practice should be stated in phrases of three to five words.
- A symbol must be associated with every rule and desired practice.
- Rules and desired practices are reviewed daily during the first month of school.
- Students must recall the rule and practice from just looking at the symbols.
- Rules that state what not to do are associated with the symbol of chaos.
- The list of desired practices is associated with the symbol of order.
- The frame and anchors should be reset periodically.
  - Resetting is the act of revisiting the experience when the frame was initially anchored or expanding on it.

Rules and Desired Practices Must Be Stated As Specific Actions

Actions are concrete; they remove the concern that an abstract concept could have multiple meanings and its application in rule making and following applied inconsistently due to interpretations or values. For example, a rule that says "Students cannot harass other students" is given to a wide range of interpretations. In one classroom, the rule means no physical contact or comment of a sexual or threatening nature; in another classroom, the same rule means no teasing. When a rule or a desired practice is stated as a specific action, it not only tells the students what not to do but also informs them of what to do. A rule identifies the action that is not appropriate. A desired practice identifies the specific behavior that is appropriate. This will mean that the rule is automatically being adhered to by the students focusing on the practices taught rather than not committing a violation. By teaching and practicing desired practices, all students will feel that they are better able to meet expectations and be successful. Just by incorporating this simple step, the anxiety of failure is reduced, lowering impulsivity.

When brainstorming rules and desired practices, it is important to reduce, then reduce, and then reduce some more. Many specific actions cover a wide range of intent. Although this will mean that some violations and practices will not be posted on the wall, it will also mean that the rules and practices that have been determined to be important can be remembered by everyone. The posting of just those limited key rules and practices is perceived by the brain to be achievable. The human brain, when allowed to focus on just a few items deemed important, will improve working memory, will have the information become more relevant, and will recall it faster (Badre and Wagner 2007, pp. 2883–2901).

A book containing hundreds of rules is seldom learned or completely followed. College athletic coaches claim that the NCAA has established so many rules that they violate them inadvertently every day. Once the concept exists that the rules are impossible to maintain, the number of violations will increase. The rules in this case become irrational and unfair. If coaches cannot maintain them even when attempting not to commit an infraction, then they will begin to view them as unachievable. Then the coaches who are a little more impulsive will commit a few small violations intentionally. Over time, the system will produce a greater number of violations. That is why when setting up classroom management, it is important to avoid the temptation to have rules for every possible violation.

Each Rule or Practice Should Be Stated in Phrases of Three to Five Words

The limited rules and desired practices developed should be stated in phrases of three to five words so that they can be attractive to the hippocampus and more easily remembered by all students. In reviewing school programs that have had difficulty being implemented, a consistent occurrence has been the inability of the staff to remember the steps of the program. As the school year proceeded, the staff began to view the program as confusing and finally not worth the hassle. For something to be adhered to, it must be easily remembered.

A Symbol Must Be Associated with Every Rule and Desired Practice

Every rule and desired practice is associated with a symbol for a few reasons. The brain is able to recognize a symbol when it is in a state of arousal. This means that in times when words are less likely to be processed by the brain, directing the student's focus to a symbol will register all of what has been taught. Symbols are also important since they themselves can become valued by the brain. Once a symbol becomes recognized and valuable to the brain, it can become a source of motivation. Then just having the symbol highly visible in the classroom can help prompt student behavior.

Rules and Desired Practices are Reviewed Daily during the First Month of School

Once rules and desired practices are established, they must be consistently reviewed and practiced. The rules and desired practices must be learned in a manner that students can recall them just by looking at the symbols. Desired practices must be performed and reinforced by making them part of a daily classroom experience. One of the problems with "don't do" rules is that the student does not practice them; they just occur in times of chemical imbalance, and then teachers attempt for the first time to have a student comply with an alternative behavior. By teaching desired practices, teachers establish alternative practices, do them when students are chemically more balanced, and have already established a practice to have it positively associated in the brain.

Rules and Desired Practices Must Be Framed and Anchored

The association of what not to do with chaos and desired practices with order is an important step. It frames why students should not do a behavior, and if appropriately anchored, it can begin to internally motivate practices. Teachers continue to believe that students all come with a clear understanding of right and wrong, and failures are therefore an act of choice. However, since chemical imbalance has such great implications on utilizing what one knows and the triggering of impulsive behaviors, knowledge can no longer be seen as a sufficient motivator during times of arousal. Many parents know that shouting and berating children is not a productive method of communication. However, when aroused, this knowledge is put aside, and emotional response takes over. A deep association of rules and orderly practices to order and balance begins to provide all students with the association of the classroom with a place that makes them feel better. This simple association improves chemical disposition in the classroom and creates a more positive perception of rules and practices.

The Frame and Anchors Should Be Reset Periodically

Once all these steps have been successfully established, teachers will need to reset the frame occasionally and anchor to remind students why they avoid negative behaviors and produce desired practices. It is important to remember that the range of a student's biopsychosocial health will determine the frequency at which frames and anchors have to be reset. For example, in a classroom with only a few students who are placed "at-risk by life's circumstances," the teacher needs to reset less often than in a classroom where most students are placed "at-risk by life's circumstances." Waiting for a violation and then stating that the student already knows right from wrong because it was established on the first day of school is contradictory to the science of teaching all students.

Anchor Points

It is reality that the students who suffer from the greatest chemical imbalances will need more than just the perception of an orderly classroom to improve their chemical disposition, which calls for some additional practices to be incorporated in the classroom. In order to improve the likelihood of success, it is important to engage in daily practices designed to improve chemical disposition. This is why classrooms must establish rituals that are consistently followed. These rituals allow the mind and body to predict and adjust to a setting. In order to perform any task, the brain and body must process a range of chemicals. It has been stated a number of times that the amygdala is alerted to differences and eased by commonality. The reaction to things that are familiar versus those that are uncommon actually relates to the chemical processing of the brain. New experiences cause the brain to process chemically at a faster rate of speed. It is the rate of speed that determines the level of emotion in a chemical experience. Familiar practices become less chemically arousing over time, and once they have become customary, they actually signal the amygdala that the events are not threatening. Over time they even become comforting to the brain. Effective classrooms for all students develop rituals to help transition students, promote desired practices and skills, and develop long-term behaviors.

The most significant chemical shifts in the school day occur during major transitions. Major transitions are times in the schedule where there is a dramatic increase in stimuli: sounds, sights, movements, etc. As was noted before, in most schools, this means admission, lunch, dismissal, hallway transitions, and all transitions associated with special or unscheduled events. Rituals allow teachers to implement a practice that is designed to lower arousal levels of each student directly prior to and after a major transition. Since common nonthreatening practices reduce the chemical reaction of the emotional brain, they are an effective tool for reducing emotional reactions.

The more unified and simplistic the rituals, the more effective they will be. For example, a schoolwide transition ritual is superior to a ritual done only by one class. The schoolwide ritual will be consistent throughout a student's tenure and provide greater opportunities for success for those who suffer greater chemical imbalance. There are some guiding principles for developing a ritual that will increase its effectiveness:

- It should be quick and easy to do.
- It should incorporate some sensory element: music, movement, catch phrase, etc.
- It should be done consistently.
- Adults must model the correct nonverbal cues when leading or participating in a ritual.
- It should be age appropriate.
- Whenever possible, the ritual should frame the activity following the ritual in a positive light.

Scientific Requirements for Establishing an Effective Ritual

- Establish a sensory procedure.
- Align to values held by the amygdala.
- Establish an associated symbol.
- Do the sensory procedure on a consistent schedule.
    - o Randomly reinforce the practice when done correctly.
    - o Celebrate consistent adherence to the procedure.

- Model the right nonverbal cues.

Establish a Sensory Procedure

Rituals are as old as man himself since they have always been a natural source of comfort. The best way to learn how to do a ritual is to recognize those we encounter all the time and note their commonalities. For example, many people go to church and know when to stand or kneel based on a music cue; they state affirmations cued by the movement, often in front of a symbol. This is in fact a sensory procedure because of the music and movement, which is framed by affirmation and anchored by symbols that have significant meaning to the parishioners. In other words, the practice makes people feel chemically better once they have engaged in the process. This simple illustration has naturally incorporated all the elements required in a good ritual. Teachers do not need to overthink this process. One good transitional ritual can be utilized prior to every transition.

Rituals need to be easy, or teachers will not maintain the practice. They need to incorporate some sensory elements so that the hippocampus and the amygdala are highly involved in the process. It is important to remember that the hippocampus processes senses independently unless they are activated consistently together. This allows for the concept or lesson to be brought back by any of the sensory elements involved. This not only improves learning but also helps the amygdala become familiar with the process because a consistent pattern of chemical movement lowers the level of arousal.

Align with Values of the Amygdala

If the ritual aligns with an inherent value of the amygdala, it will increase the importance of the ritual. Most people are aware that their values are an outcome of life experiences. The experiences that shape our values the most are emotional ones. This means the strongest-held values are an outcome of both positive and negative experiences. The reality in the brain is that the more emotional the experience, the faster the chemical movement and the greater its impact on behavior. As a result, the experiences that have the greatest impact on behavior are usually traumatic. That is because trauma produces the highest rate of chemical movement in the brain automatically. Therefore, it is not surprising that most people know at least one individual who experienced a trauma that immediately changed his/her behavior. On the other hand, positive experiences seldom have as significant an impact on the chemical speed of the brain. That is why most positive values are associated with repetitive practices that one engaged in growing up. The repetition of a positive practice over time increases the speed, thereby increasing the value.

Teachers were misled to believe that rewards were a means to change behavior when they unknowingly had merely stumbled onto something that a student already valued. However, since every student did not share in the same experiences while growing up, the reward was not effective with everyone. Even so, everyone's amygdala shares three inherent values: the need to be safe, wanted, and successful. It is recommended that teachers focus on aligning sensory procedures to one of these values to ensure universal appeal.

Establish an Associated Symbol

One of the most consistently heard complaints made by teachers is that they have difficulty in motivating students to engage in newly taught practices. For this reason, developing a symbol that is associated with the sensory procedure is crucial. Motivation begins in the preorbital frontal cortex. This part of the brain secretes a specific form of dopamine that is associated with human motivation. The preorbital frontal cortex most readily recognizes symbols associated with things valued by the amygdala. Adding a symbol to a procedure can help in the process of motivating students. However, it is important not just to create a symbol but to make sure that it is automatically associated with the procedure and repeated over time. The student must see the symbol and think of the specific procedure.

Do the Sensory Procedure on a Consistent Schedule

If a practice has sensory features, is valued by the amygdala, and has some symbolic representation, it has all the elements necessary for the reward pathway to respond. The reward pathway is responsible for making new practices become consistent behaviors. When all the correct elements are in place, the reward pathway will begin to secrete dopamine along the nucleus accumbens, resulting in a new, persistent practice. Many students who are not able to develop a new practice easily often suffer from damaged reward pathways. Thus, it is also recommended that two additional techniques that improve dopamine flow be incorporated to increase the production. The nucleus accumbens has a dopamine response to tangible rewards. However, the science states that it must be randomized and cannot take the place of the consistency, which is what the brain is truly designed to reinforce. In addition, recognition can also periodically produce dopamine in the nucleus accumbens. However, recognition has to be something anticipated. When using recognition, it is important to have some buildup to the event in order to increase the chances of a dopamine response.

Model the Right Nonverbal Cues

When a new practice involves social behavior, the amygdala will monitor man's inherent nonverbal cues in order to see if they are consistent with what is being said or done. Remember, the amygdala monitors facial expressions, hand gestures, body postures, and tone of voice. For example, a mother has established a very productive ritual for putting her son to bed. Every evening she goes to the clock on the wall and says, "The small hand is on the number 8, and the big hand is on the number 12, so the clock on the wall says?" And the child responds, "It is time to go to bed." "Do your three steps and I will read you a story for each step." The child then washes his face, brushes his teeth, and puts on his pajamas. Then Mother meets him at his bed, turns down the light, and reads him three stories. The child's amygdala inherently knows that this is a calm time in which his mother reads in a melodic voice, smiles, and says I love you and kisses him good night. The amygdala monitors for a calm voice tone and loving facial demeanor, relaxed body posture, and slow, smooth gestures. If mother were to sound angry, look upset, sit in a tense position, or move abruptly when saying good night, this would hamper the brain's ability to produce the normal dopamine response to the ritual. The conclusion is that human behavior must logically match the tone of the ritual that is being carried out. It is adult behavior that is the glue of rituals designed to teach social behaviors and produce a safe and nurturing environment.

Social Needs

Since the amygdala watches man in all group settings, it is also important to improve social comfort in the classroom setting. We have learned that the amygdala is alerted to differences and eased by commonality. Therefore, an effective method for improving the relationship among students is to improve the amygdala's awareness of things students have in common while reframing differences. A phrase I like to use is "We are all uniquely the same." I tell students that our brains and bodies share so much in common that we can explain even the most dramatic differences based on some unique occurrence. In order for the amygdala to remain calm, it is important to stress commonalities rather than accentuate differences. Even when variances occur, they are usually not all that unique since others sharing similar traits and experiences will produce similar patterns. This is the premise of diagnosis.

The easiest way to achieve social comfort is to have students participate in activities that draw attention to nonthreatening things they share with others in the classroom. For example, there are students from inner city to rural areas, rich to poor, Protestant to Catholic that all like basketball, the color red, hamburgers, and fast cars. The amygdala is drawn toward others who share outward and then inward similarities. Natural group dynamics produce separation due to the brain's need for safety and comfort. Then when under stress, those points of demarcation with other students will become a source of irritation. Those students suffering from the greatest chemical imbalances will behave more impulsively and aggressively toward those who are the most different. Once the differences have been openly identified and have become a source of irritation, group dynamics will be negatively impacted.

The practice of placing students into groups based on things they share in common will help the amygdala focus on similarities rather than irritating differences. Teachers can survey students at the beginning of the school year in order to collect a wide range of information that can be manipulated during group projects. During the first three weeks of school, each teacher can then have every student be part of a different group based on things they share in common. The goal is that over the first three weeks of school, each student will have worked on a group project with every member of the classroom and be alerted each time as to what they share in common. For example, Susan, Billy, John, and Rick were selected to work on a project because their favorite color is purple. The next project Susan works with Reggie, Paul, Martin, and David because their favorite food is pizza. On the third project Susan is paired with Thomas, Sally, Sam, and Mary because they all play a musical instrument. This process is repeated until all students have worked in a cooperative manner with all the other students while learning that they share things in common with everyone in the classroom.

Before teachers have students work on group projects, however, they must teach and practice the guidelines for group processing. These guidelines will be used all year and are principles that students must not only learn but also value enough to shape behaviors. This means that group-processing guidelines must meet all the steps for creating new long-term behavioral change: sensory procedure, valued by the amygdala, symbol association, and consistent practice.

Group-processing guidelines

1. Everyone has skills.
   a. It's the group's job to find out how to best use those skills.

2. Make a plan – everyone contributes an idea – no bad ideas.
   a. What has to be done?

3. Assign tasks – everyone participates – volunteer.
   a. I will do . . .

4. Put together – each person succeeds – the team succeeds.
   a. The task is to put it all together.

One of the most effective methods for teaching good group-processing skills is to have the group naturally develop them through a range of short preassignment activities. A preassignment activity is a task that provides the group with an action or a problem that they must complete by working together. It can be as simple as having each member of the group keep a balloon in the air until each team member has touched it. Then additional elements can be added that force the team to have to work together. For example, you can have each team member be able to touch the balloon only once, with only the body part you call out, and group members must organize themselves without talking. The groups will quickly organize themselves and figure out how to best achieve each task.

Next, the teacher has the group process how they accomplished the task and identify how the skills they used to achieve the activity will help them with the next assignment. The skills should be written down and posted. Then the teacher should emphasize to the students that since they accomplished the first activity, they will certainly succeed in the next one. These preassignment activities do not take long and are a good way to have students realize through experience all the group processing guidelines. Preassignment activities should be repeated before each group task until the class has identified every skill the teacher has predetermined. Many teachers find this such an easy way to transition groups into doing their assignments that they maintain the practice as a consistent classroom strategy.

Transition Ritual and Consistently Used Skills

Teachers might find the need to establish an in-class transition ritual. In-class transition rituals are especially useful if a teacher has the same students for the majority of the school day, or if he or she has a class that has a significant number of students with behavioral problems. Students who consistently demonstrate behavioral issues often come to school experiencing a certain level of chemical imbalance. In a high stimuli setting such as school and a classroom, these students' imbalances begin to mount throughout the day. As a result, these students can struggle during each transition within a classroom, especially if transitioning to a subject matter that they find challenging or have had a history of failure with.

In-class transition rituals should be accomplished successfully in a matter of seconds. The ritual should still seek to meet the elements within the science but in an expedited fashion. Below is an example of an in-class transition ritual:

- Music cue plays.
- Teacher snaps her fingers and says with the catch phrase, "It's time to do . . ."
- Then the students all say the scheduled activity, "Math."
- Then the teacher snaps her fingers again and says, "That's OK, you'll do . . ."
- Then students all pump their fist up in the air while saying, "Great!"

A quick review of this in-class transition ritual reveals that although it is brief, it meets all the requirements if done correctly. The teacher must have a class schedule. The schedule must be taught, preferably in a brain-compatible manner until all the students can quickly recall the class agenda. Then a symbol must be associated with the transition. The symbol should represent in students' minds, "It is time to make a transition." The teacher should post the symbol near the CD player where she cues the music. Then the transition should be initiated by her tapping the symbol three times and then cueing the music. The above mentioned in-class transition ritual would then begin.

The in-class transition ritual has many sensory elements grouped together: music, movement, and catch phrases. It is aligned with the value held by the amygdala, success. The ritual has a visual cue. Therefore, all the teacher has to do is model the nonverbal behaviors that should be logically expected by the brain, and the required elements have been met in a matter of seconds. It is important to note that meeting the steps outlined in the science can be done very efficiently. The seconds invested to ease into transitions are rewarded by the reduction of impulsive behaviors.

Another place teachers might want to establish a consistent ritual is for a set of skills that students will have to utilize regularly. Most classes establish a test-taking procedure. A test-taking procedure recognizes that if students become anxious before taking a test, their ability to think and remember will be hampered. In addition, if students do not have a strategy for attacking a test, then they are more likely to become frustrated if they cannot answer the first few questions on an exam. Once anxiety is heightened, the brain's ability to process and remember becomes increasingly compromised. Think about playing a memory game and knowing you know the answer but not being able to recall the information on demand. It seems that the more you try, the harder it gets. Then once the pressure is off, you remember. A test-taking ritual is a good skill to teach all students to help them have sound strategies that they will utilize throughout their academic careers.

The test-taking ritual should be instituted by following the science established below:

- Establish a sensory procedure.
- Align to values held by the amygdala.
- Establish an associated symbol.
- Repeat the sensory procedure on a regular schedule.
  - o Randomly reinforce the practice when done correctly.
  - o Celebrate consistent adherence to the procedure.

- Model the right nonverbal cues.

A teacher can easily frame and anchor the test-taking procedure. See the script below for an example:

The teacher is playing the theme song from Mission Impossible in the background. She gathers the students together and instructs them to close the classroom door and pay close attention. In a whispering voice she tells them, "I am going to give you the secret of how to do better on every test you take for the rest of your life. So when I bring my finger to my mouth, it will be your cue to use the test-taking secrets you will learn." This has framed the test-taking ritual.

The teacher then anchors the ritual by associating each step to a physical posture done when someone is excited and has accomplished some great task: the throwing up of both fists in the air. The teacher sets the stage by saying, "And for each secret step, I will give you one bonus point" while throwing her arms in the air. Here are the "seven secret steps":

- **Step 1** – Write "I will do my best" on the top of the page.
  - o The teacher says, "And if you write it, you will get," and the students say while throwing their hands in the air, "One free bonus point."

- **Step 2** – Quickly review the whole test and place a check next to the questions that you think you know the most about.
- ☑ The teacher says, "And if you write the checks, you will get," and the students say while throwing their hands in the air, "One free bonus point."

- **Step 3** –
  - ★ Place a star next to the questions with the highest value.
  - O Place a circle next to the questions with the next highest value.
  - – Place a line next to the questions with the next highest value.
- ★ O – The teacher says, "And if you write the stars, circle, and lines in the right places, you will get," and the students all say while throwing their hands in the air, "One free bonus point."

- **Step 4** – Read the directions carefully in the section with the highest value where you have at least one check mark. Underline the key words in the directions as you read.
  - o The teacher says, "And if you underline the key words of the directions, you will get," and the students all say while throwing their hands in the air, "One free bonus point."

- **Step 5** – Repeat step 4 in the section with the next highest value where you have at least one check mark until you have completed the test.
- **Step 6** – Attempt to do as many of the other questions as possible.
  - o The teacher says, "And if you answer all the questions, you will get," and the students all say while throwing their hands in the air, "One free bonus point."

- **Step 7** – If you have extra time, check over the test.

Many of the elements in this test-taking ritual are based on brain science. The ritual begins by consistently establishing a positive perception: "I will do my best." Positive perceptions have been found to help improve the chemical functioning of the brain. There is a visual cue, which is the teacher bringing her index finger in front of her mouth and making the "shh" sound. The next step has the students instantly focus on the elements in the test they are most familiar with. By having the students look for and place a check beside the questions that they think they know, they can attack the test before looking at any questions that will produce the frustration incurred in not knowing. By the time the student is attempting to answer questions that they are not as familiar with, other related files in the brain have had an opportunity to open. This will improve the probability that the students will maximize what they have learned.

The teacher still has to teach the test-taking ritual in a brain-compatible manner in order to ensure that each student can remember the steps. This means that each step should be reduced to a catch phrase, each step assigned a symbol; each step needs to be reviewed until students can recall it by only looking at the symbols. Then the teacher can instruct the students that they can recall the seven secret steps by just envisioning the symbols in their minds.

- **Step 1** – Write "I will do my best."
- **Step 2** – Put checks next to what I know best.
- **Step 3** – Put stars, circle, and lines.
- **Step 4** – Read directions and underline.
- **Step 5** – Answer questions with checks.
    o Start with stars, then circles, then lines.

- **Step 6** – Answer all that you can.
- **Step 7** – Check the test over.

This test-taking ritual is in fact a new behavior that can easily become a persistent practice rewarded by the brain. The teacher already has created all the elements required to make this a new, persistent practice that students will do long after they leave this class. The test-taking ritual is already a sensory procedure. The ritual is aligned with a value of the amygdala, success. The gesture of bringing the index figure to her lips provides a visual cue. The practice will be done in a consistent manner if it is practiced each time the students take a test. It can even get tangible reinforcement when students receive a good grade. Also, if the class does any celebration for individuals who have performed well consistently throughout the grading period, then every recommended reinforcement strategy has been met.

This test-taking ritual is merely an example of how you can utilize the model to address developing changes in behaviors related to academic performance. It is important to recognize that one of the most recurring findings related to students who do well at school is that they have habits in things like work organization, note taking, studying, completing homework, and test taking. Teachers can begin to address these issues early in every student's academic career. Imagine how different education would be if more students knew the skills required to be successful and practiced them until they became behaviors that students are self-motivated to perform. Many discipline issues that schools face stem from the inability of students to be successful in academic pursuits.

CHAPTER 15

Discipline

*Wise teachers create an environment that encourages
students to teach themselves.*

– Leonard Roy Frank

In the previous chapter, some of the complexities of school discipline were addressed. *Discipline* in this context simply means *the planned response to inappropriate behaviors.* The overall health, temperament, and experiences of each individual factor into how he or she will respond to every situation and how effective every intervention will be. There are students who lack the capacity to change until their overall level of health improves, while there are other students who can benefit from being taught what to do and internalize the practice right away. It is this *range* of student responses that has confused educators into believing that a successful strategy with one student will be effective with all students. However, all behavioral change is not created equal. No one should expect the bully with multiple emotional disorders and a history of exposure to violence to change as rapidly as the healthy student who engages in bullying behaviors because of peer influence. Therefore, an effective discipline plan must be able to address the full range of students and problems in order for a school to be successful in the area of discipline.

Build Capacity

Capacity refers to obtaining the level of health required not to continue engaging in habitual negative practices. One of the best ways to understand the concept of capacity is to associate it to a twelve-step substance abuse program. Twelve-steps is an approach that has had success with individuals suffering from the disease of addiction. People struggling with addiction discovered that a range of seemingly unrelated things helped their ability not to relapse: like having a mentor, improving their diet, attending church, and developing empathy, just to mention a few. The conclusion was that overcoming a chronic problem could not be achieved by simply focusing on the problem. The recovery demanded that the whole person improve. It was the new, improved individual who would have a better opportunity not to succumb to impulses. Now we know that many of these improvements are actually protective factors that are shown to help with all presenting problems.

Resiliency studies have shown that regardless of disability or presenting problems, an individual's capacity can be improved by acquiring protective factors. Since so many schools across the nation already have instituted some form of character education program, it would be easy to focus on building protective factors through these programs. Schools wishing to increase resiliency should seek to emphasize only the aspects of the character education curriculum that focus on building protective factors. It is protective factors that are found in the research to improve life outcomes. In addition to teaching identified protective factors, schools should seek to develop practices that institutionalize specific behaviors related to each protective factor. It is not enough to learn about a protective factor like empathy; it must be translated into a specific action in order to help the concept become internalized in the brain. Schools should seek to focus on building a certain protective factor each year a student is enrolled and continue to build on each one gained. These additions will provide schools with the assurance that students will become more capable in meeting behavioral expectations each year they are enrolled.

A simple approach that schools could use to promote resiliency is to focus on building one protective factor at every grade level. Each grade level is assigned a specific protective factor and one action that will be expected of that student not only during that year but also during all subsequent years he or she is enrolled in that school system. By focusing on the action, the brain is allowed to make dramatic change related to a learned concept. That is because behavioral change is found to have a more profound impact on improving brain structure than the mere learning of a fact. This approach will also offer a level of simplicity and continuity for system wide implementation. Grade-level teachers need only become proficient in promoting one protective factor and leaning all the behavioral expectations that should be in evidence at each grade level. Students new to the system are likely to learn the behavioral expectations because all students perform them without much external support. This means that a student could conceivably gain twelve or more protective factors throughout his/her educational tenure. That many protective factors could result in someone with chronic issues and a poor probability for success significantly improving his life outcomes. In addition, this approach will enable schools to take a proactive approach to teaching desired practices rather than merely punishing inappropriate behaviors. If a discipline program does not address capacity building, the staff will quickly become frustrated by the limited improvements that are made by the habitual offenders.

Language-Based Processing

Most schools formally or informally have in place some language-based processing model for dealing with inappropriate behaviors. These models seek to help students realize what behaviors are inappropriate and help them identify what alternative behaviors they could do in the future. This approach is fine when coupled with strategies for building capacity. Students who are capable of change will learn what they should be doing and eventually change their behaviors, and those who lack capacity will cognitively learn what they should do when they are able.

However, many schools utilize only a language-based processing model. The repeated complaint made by staff is that the habitual offender cognitively knows what to do but continually fails to do it. Some staff members start to believe that the same students are manipulating the process. In schools that have incorporated a language-based processing model, staff often disagree over the approach. Some staff believe in the model and perceive that the failures are a result of poor application on the part of certain teachers. The other staff believe that the model cannot work with students who exhibit severe behavioral problems. Schools must have in place models that address the range of student profiles. Brain science teaches us that cognitive knowledge is not sufficient in and of itself to make behavioral change. Therefore, utilizing only a language-based processing approach even when supported by a range of consequences will produce mixed results at best.

The Science of Establishing a New, Persistent Practice

Schools also must have the ability to implement more immediate behavioral change with students with limited capacities. This book has dedicated a significant number of pages to designing a new practice so that it is reinforced in the reward pathway. This science can be applied whenever there is a behavioral problem that requires more immediate intervention. Schools should keep data on the nature and frequency of behavioral infractions. The data should drive the discussion on discipline. This is important because discipline tends to be an emotional issue, and emotionality lowers logic and reasoning. Whenever a certain infraction is occurring at a high frequency, the staff can decide if they think the problem warrants the implementation of an alternative behavior practice. In these cases, staff will be motivated in designing the new behavior and maintaining the required element found in the science.

The discipline continuum outlined above will help schools develop a valid model for addressing the full range of behavioral problems and profiles. It also helps staff know that they are always working on the habitual problem while still teaching desired practices daily. In addition, students who are capable will still learn and change while their peers with more significant issues will continue to build capacity. In addition, schools will always have at their disposal a method for creating new, persistent behaviors to address pressing behavioral problems: the science of creating a new, persistent practice.

- Establish a sensory procedure.
- Align to values held by the amygdala.
- Establish an associated symbol.
- Repeat the sensory procedure on a regular schedule.
  - Randomly reinforce the practice when done correctly.
  - Celebrate consistent adherence to the procedure.
- Model the right nonverbal cues.

By now readers should be clear on the fact that brain science should be used to respond to both behavioral and academic issues. The two are so intertwined that it is impossible to completely separate one from the other. Although this chapter spoke only on the behavior, it is safe to assume that many times, negative actions are triggered by issues related to learning. The same approach used to develop a new alternative behavior is the same one used to develop a long-term academic practice. Discipline within an educational context should never be separated from instruction and curriculum implementation.

CHAPTER 16

A Brain-Based Approach to Curriculum Implementation

Give the pupils something to do, not something to learn; and the doing is of such a nature as to demand thinking; learning naturally results.

– John Dewey

In the world of high-stakes testing, brain-based teaching strategies must be implemented in a manner that is efficient and produces consistent gains on standardized exams. Some people claim that such an approach is tantamount to "teaching to the test." However, there are some facts concerning the range of brain function for students in most classes that cannot be ignored. Students suffering from emotional problems, cognitive deficits, and daily stress consistently perform lower on language-based testing. That is because chemical imbalance in the brain reduces language processing. A brain-based method designed to overcome language deficits is required if schools are to make advances with every student. It is only logical to implement these methods when teaching materials that will be required before students can pass standardized tests since it is these tests that often determine matriculation to the next grade, access to advanced courses, and represent the skill sets needed for high performance on college entrance exams.

STEP 1: Identify Quintessential Facts

Teachers first need to identify the quintessential facts that are expectations of standardized testing in their subject area. This does not mean all the facts that the teacher would like the student to learn, but those that are the most essential to performing well on standardized tests. These facts must be taught following the brain-based strategies identified earlier in the book. Each fact should be reduced to a catch phase, associated with a symbol, and reviewed regularly while doing an identified physical motion. The goal is for students to increase the speed of recall. For example, if teaching a section on the hippocampus and the amygdala, the teacher would determine the quintessential facts that must be recalled quickly. Once the facts are identified, they should be reduced to a catch phrase and assigned a symbol:

 The amygdala controls emotions.

 The hippocampus controls learning.

The students will make an almond shape with the hand whenever they say the catch phrase related to the amygdala and a horseshoe shape with their hand whenever they say the catch phrase related to the hippocampus. After the students have reviewed these facts enough to indicate an improvement in the speed of recall, the catch phrase should be omitted from the review process, leaving only the motions and the symbols. See example below:

There are many reasons for having the information triggered by a symbol. There is strong historical evidence that man is able to remember large amounts of information triggered only by a symbol. Also, the amygdala resonates to symbols. This means that even if the person becomes aroused, the amygdala can trigger information when seeing a symbol. In addition, children in advanced cultures spend large amounts of time refining this ability. The media utilize symbols to represent most products in commercials. Many students can identify thousands of products by the symbol alone. Students can even be taught to recall the information imagining what the symbol looks like.

In addition to the incorporation of a symbol, it is important to focus on increasing speed. There are two reasons to increase speed. One is myelination. Myelination is the "white matter" that insulates neurons and increases speed. A myelin sheath increases the speed at which impulses propagate along the fiber. The increased speed of impulses improves recall. The other reason to increase speed is to improve memory function when under stress. About thirty years ago at Cornell University Medical College, Joseph LeDoux was studying emotional memories. He determined that when individuals become aroused, there are two pathways to accessing memory. One stream of thought goes toward the cortex where it is integrated with other real-time sensory data. He coined this stream the high road. The other stream of thought goes toward the amygdala in an instantaneous fashion at a high rate of speed. This he called the low road. It was determined that memory stored at a higher speed becomes available for instantaneous access in times of high emotion. In contrast, memories stored in the cortex are accessed at a much-slower rate of speed. Therefore, information stored at a higher rate of speed can become similar to automated responses that occur even when under duress. In turn, this process can trigger access to other associated information that has been learned.

Teachers should seek to implement a consistent review process. The dedicating of the first five to ten minutes of each class to review will solidify learning. This is why the most advanced research on reading instruction drills students on phonemic awareness the first five minutes of each class. Teachers should not focus on instructional time lost, but rather on how much more efficient learning will be if the cornerstones of the curriculum are known by all students instantaneously. These facts can also become constant sources of reference that the teacher knows each student understands. This will ensure that teachers can build on what the students already know. It also allows the teacher to appeal to students who learn at a different pace not to become despondent. Teachers can inform these students that all the information that they will need to do well in end-of-year testing will be reviewed so frequently that they will eventually learn it. This encouragement will provide struggling students with the motivation to continue and not become behavioral problems because of frustrations over academic performance.

There are two approaches to implementing this brain-based curriculum implementation model. The first is to identify all the significant facts and develop catch phrases, symbols, unique movements, and consistent time for review before each school year. This ensures that no key facts will be missed and that only the most significant items are identified. The second approach is to identify each fact as it occurs in each lesson. The weakness of this approach is that facts are more likely to be missed, and there will be less opportunity to create good catch phrases and identify appropriate symbols. There is one additional option available to teachers who engage in group instruction. The group-instruction process has the collective body of students take control of the learning process and teach one another. In this type of classroom the students are taught how to identify key facts, develop their own catch phrases and movements, and even lead the review process.

Two Approaches to Curriculum Implementation

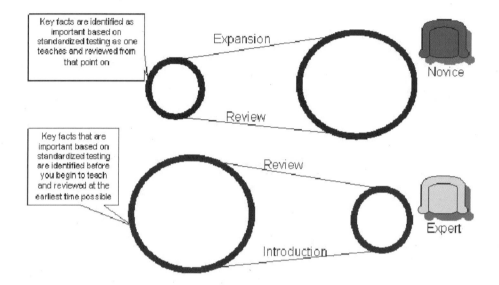

STEP 2: Get Student Focus

The human brain requires sensory focus in order to activate attention, solution, problem solving, and appropriate response. Many teachers introduce challenging new topics and assume that every student is focused and comprehending. Nothing could be farther from the truth. Students with a history of academic failure and those with limited exposure and experiences to aid in comprehension often require transitional activities to help them activate the sensory process and begin to draw connections with the information being taught.

There are two recommendations for transitioning into challenging new lessons: comprehension activity and comprehension experience.

Comprehension Activity

- Any activity activating a range of senses and actions that begins to help the student focus on a task in order to transition into the lesson
  - o Helps students transition
  - o Is able to be managed by those suffering from chemical imbalances
  - o Helps students make loose correlations between the lesson and the world

When teaching the lesson about the amygdala, which controls emotion, a teacher could have students look at videos in which people demonstrate strong emotions and attempt to identify what emotion was being exhibited. Then transition into the lesson by explaining that students will now learn about the part of the brain that produces these emotions. The comprehension activity provides a bridge from a sensory-activating activity to the challenging new subject matter.

Comprehension Experience

- Any activity through which an individual can gain a more comprehensive understanding of something new through a range of senses
  - Builds on what people know the most about
  - Is able to be managed by those suffering from chemical imbalances
  - Creates long-term potentiation
  - Helps students make correlations with the world

The comprehension experience not only transitions into the lesson but also is an active part of the lesson. When teaching about the hippocampus, the teacher has the students conduct a series of memory experiments to determine what seems to improve memory. Each experiment is designed to identify a rule for helping the hippocampus focus and recall. Students work in pairs and are given instructions on how to conduct each experience and then to write a rule on how the hippocampus learns best. For example, one card instructs one student to show his partner a series of numbers and then have him write the numbers down after a certain amount of time has elapsed: 1030497042, 2048-47720, and 018-473-4667. Most students will recall the number sequence that has three small groupings the best. The rule would be that the hippocampus prefers smaller groupings. The comprehension experience not only transitioned students into the lesson but also carried the students through the lesson. Teachers find that this is a more advanced skill than just creating a related activity to introduce new material.

Both comprehension activities and experiences are strongly recommended for the introduction of challenging new subject matter. This is when a higher number of students might not have the background to comprehend the lesson and are at greater risk of not focusing. Once teachers get used to using these strategies, they will find them a good teaching practice to increase student attention and reduce negative behaviors. It is important to note that when comprehension experiences are used, they improve comprehension. However, when comprehension activities are used, the teacher needs to make correlations between the lesson and what the students know well.

STEP 3: Identify Skills That Must Be Consistently Applied
Since skill sets refer to learned behaviors, they should be taught as if designing a new, persistent behavior. The goal here is to teach only the most vital skills so that they will not only be remembered but also be applied. The book has dedicated a great deal

of time outlining and illustrating how to apply the science on this topic. Therefore, rather than reviewing the science yet again, it might be important to help teachers determine if a skill should be taught in this fashion. Ask the following questions to make that decision:

- Will the skill be utilized consistently throughout the school year?
- Does the skill need to be applied for students to do well on standardized testing?
- Is the skill a cornerstone of the curriculum?

The recommendations in this chapter do not prescribe a dramatic change in instruction but rather suggest modifications that can be applied systemically across grade levels and student populations. However, the science identified in this book reveals that administrators and teachers alike will have to learn to value these modifications and develop structures that reinforce these practices. In addition, schools must focus their attention on structuring not only the classroom and the school but also on the entire organization in order to promote consistent quality education throughout a district.

CHAPTER 17

The New Science of Systems Change and Analysis

Great minds have always encountered violent opposition from mediocre minds.
– Albert Einstein

It is the application of neuroscience to the understanding of systems theory that will enable education to implement successful programmatic redesign. First of all, we must keep in mind that institutions are merely a collection of individuals. Systems analysis has traditionally focused on system functions rather than the various profiles of individuals that account for the range of human behavior. This traditional approach will always yield inconsistent findings because it fails to account for variables in human behavior while continuing to design policies and procedures to address individual conduct. Policies and procedures impact various human profiles differently, producing diverse behaviors. Any valid systems theory must be able to account for how behavioral variances will be addressed, how group dynamics will influence individual behavior, and how various profiles will respond to certain institutional practices. In order to implement change, administrators in the field of education must shift focus from systems function to human function.

Institutions that have been in existence for long periods of time inevitably seek to standardize certain practices in an attempt to structure tasks and predict performance and output. It is this approach that laid the foundation for the current group-management style normally implemented in institutions within Western culture. Simply put, institutions sought to establish universal expectations in order to achieve uniform practices. An example of a uniform practice is "every employee must report to work by 8:00 am." Group expectations soon led to standardized policies and procedures. Over time, institutions began to utilize policies and procedures as a method for dealing with individual personnel issues within larger organizations.

In the evolution of any large institution, individual behaviors occur that are not predicted or planned for. An employee demonstrates a behavior not done previously by other members of the group. In the case of a small organization, such behavioral variances are dealt with directly with the individual. However, when a similar behavior occurs in a larger institution, the concern is that the behavior might occur again; in a large institution, the sheer numbers of employees increase the risk that the behavior might be repeated. The fear is that an ill-advised practice might reach epidemic proportions. Many times this fear is unfounded. However, the use of policies and procedures as an effective approach for governing group behavior seems to focus on preventing the worst-case scenario. This approach supersedes the logic that many behaviors are just isolated incidents. It is at this stage in institutional development that policies and procedures became an accepted method for dealing with human behavioral variance. For example, a state employee utilizes the company car to run personal errands. She is seen shopping at the local grocery store by a taxpaying citizen, and a complaint is filed. In order to prevent this behavior from happening in the future, the institution invokes a new policy that no employee should drive a state vehicle to go to stores or a shopping mall.

The rule, although well-meaning, has unforeseen consequences. The policy eliminates a number of eateries that a state employee can go to while carrying out his duties throughout the state. In addition, state employees who spend a high percentage of time on the road often need to replenish personal items that have run out or were forgotten. In these cases, stopping at a store is job related but still against policy. As a result, a small number of state employees will ignore the rule because they perceive it as extreme. This attitude places these employees at risk for committing violations that jeopardize their employment. Most state employees obey the rule but are forced to violate it in certain cases, such as traveling to small towns where every restaurant is located in a strip mall. However, there are a few state employees who will never violate the rule because the breach will cause them greater anxiety than going through extreme measures to avoid committing a related infraction. The individuals who never violate this rule increase the probability that they will never be reprimanded or be at odds with state policy. This scenario clearly illustrates how different individuals react differently to the same policy or procedure. More importantly, the example illustrates that certain individual profiles are more likely to adhere to even irrational policies and procedures due to their neurobiology.

Over the history of established institution, many rules came into existence as a response to isolated infractions committed by one individual. These rules then become part of the policies and procedures manual. Over time, new employees are expected to learn these rules when hired to avoid inadvertently violating policy. Some new employees will view many of these rules as irrational since they are not aware of the context in which they were developed. Agencies will require these employees to sign documents stating that they will uphold the rules that they have read. It is at this moment in an agency's evolution that the ability to value agency rules becomes a visible indicator of a good employee. The employee whose values align with those of the institution will be promoted. The aligning of values becomes important in larger institutions because the emphasis is placed on the modeling of similar practices; individualism will be viewed as a negative behavior. Those individuals whose chemical dispositions seek out extensive rules and protocols will soon be drawn to the structure offered by such agencies. They will even begin to value the agency status symbols. Remember, symbols can take on enormous emotional value. These individuals will aspire to a closer parking space to the office, having a cubicle with a window, receiving the gold watch given at retirement. Those whose neurobiological makeup is helped by such a structured environment will desire long-term affiliation (because they do not like change). Maintaining employment will take on such importance that the thought of jeopardizing their job by committing even a justified infraction will be unfathomable.

It is important to look at how the neurobiology of human behavior applies to institutional practices. Mirror neurons are a subset of neurons in the brain-motor areas that reflect in the observer's brain those acts performed by others (Rizzolatti et al. 2006). Sets of mirror neurons appear to encode templates for specific actions in the brain. As a result, mirror neurons serve to teach and encode a range of behavioral functions. The range of behaviors that mirror neurons respond to are the behaviors most likely learned and replicated. It is therefore important to know what mirror neurons respond to: they respond most intensely to replicate pattern behaviors related to survival (eating, drinking, sex, and things associated to livelihood). Therefore, mirror neurons will note practices demonstrated by the group at lunchtime. This explains why in large institutions, behavioral patterns surrounding lunch become so easily entrenched. Mirror neurons respond to social behaviors that are intuitive to the amygdala (facial expressions, body postures, gestures, hand movement, and nervous repetitive behaviors). This means that human emotions related to behavioral practices are also taught and emulated. Mirror neurons respond to a range of actions that relate to social interaction within a group. Once a group has developed a behavioral practice, the fact that so many people do it will increase compliance. That is because the action is played several times a day in the brain. These mirror neurons appear to have the ability to confer intentions of the behaviors of others. In other words, mirror neurons will not only predict the behavior but also assume the intent of the action.

Once a behavioral protocol in an institution becomes consistently modeled, it will become the pervasive pattern of the majority. Consistently seeing the practice is as influential as doing the behavior oneself. Mirror neurons will replay identified behavioral patterns each day for the duration of employment. When a variant behavior occurs, the sheer difference will cause the brain to focus because it does not match the established visual pattern. When the work climate becomes stressful, the unique behavior will become a source of irritation to the majority. The emotional response of the majority to the individualized practice will become evident through facial expressions, postures, and gestures of the majority. This begins to explain why even small behavioral violations can be viewed with such disdain within large institutions.

Individuals with difficult temperaments who suffer from mild chemical imbalance will seek out the structure provided by highly structured institutions. However, they, too, will struggle with any change to rules and procedures that they have grown accustomed to. Those possessing shy and anxious temperaments also will be drawn to highly structured environments. Together, these two profiles become pervasive in these types of institutions because the institution offers them what they need and because they do not want to experience change. In addition, these temperaments will increase their comfort by surrounding themselves with others who reflect their own behaviors and attitudes.

Two outcomes occur in highly structured institutions: those who desire structure will seek out the institution, and those who value the rules of the institution will be elevated to roles of leadership. The moment an individual enters a new social group, he or she first seeks the safety and comfort of those who are most like himself. Remember, the amygdala likes itself the most. Individuals who have superior chemical balance, easier temperaments, and good exposure will usually get along with a wider range of behavioral profiles but will tend to be more flexible in regard to social protocols. They tend to accept a wider range of methods to achieve a desired result. Their level of tolerance prevents them from seeing many things as black or white. Those who suffer from some chemical imbalance and have more difficult or shy temperaments will have a more narrow range of compatible colleagues and will tend to be less flexible in regard to social protocols.

Over time, the number of employees who value the structure of the institution will increase because they will be drawn to the institution and what it represents. In addition, since the amygdala likes itself, when these individuals engage in hiring new employees, they will tend to select others who are like themselves. Occasionally, the institution will make a mistake and hire a person who will not take the policies and procedures too seriously. However, this individual will find himself at constant odds with each new policy and with his fellow employees who not only seem to adhere to the rules but also seem to display nonverbal signs of their displeasure with his or her behavior.

When stress rises in the institutional setting, individuals who share the least in common with the majority will become targets because of their behavioral variances. Anyone, too, outside the norm will feel pressure to conform or become further displaced. After a while, the institution will develop rigid policies that will make dramatic change less likely. The chance that change will occur will become less likely because consistency will be what the personality types in power desire most. Change, when it comes, will come incrementally and with extensive scrutiny. The outcome will be that the institution will produce very little variance. Even when new initiatives are launched, they will look strangely familiar because they will tend to have a lot of familiar themes and elements. This is the primary reason why education continually purchases failed programs. In reality, education has become one of the largest institutions in the world. Traditional practices long associated with education are constantly reinvented. When seeking to try new things, education is subconsciously drawn to the same failed methods with some new but unthreatening element added. What is produced is merely incremental change in a dynamic world, leaving Western education always attempting to solve age-old problems with age-old solutions. This is the reason why dynamic agencies such as Microsoft sought to reinvent themselves once they had become too big. They could no longer make quick decisions in a dynamic market. So they broke themselves down into smaller companies, seeking to recapture the magic and creativity that made them pioneers in their field.

Perhaps no other institutions are more at odds with their mandates than institutions of higher learning. It is here that young minds are supposed to be exposed to a wide range of ideas in order to create sound, independent thinkers. The problem is that universities have become some of the oldest and largest institutions in the world. The reputation of many of these institutions is that for even a minor change to take place, an exhaustive process must be undertaken. This is logical because in no other place do we find such a large collection of highly intelligent personalities that are comfortable in highly structured environments. Therefore, change itself must withstand intellectual scrutiny that tends to defend whatever is already in existence. That is why changes to the curriculum in many of these institutions are so difficult and time-consuming. The common perception is that these institutions become out of touch with the very professions they train students to enter.

However, there are many universities that are known for producing independent thinkers and cutting-edge change across fields of study. In these universities, the goals of development and discovery are most valued. If we look closely, we can see clearly that the institutional policies and procedures have been brought into alignment with these values. The initial screening process attracts smart, independent thinkers and visionaries. The curriculum promotes new ideas when evaluating what has been studied for ages. Many department policies seek to ensure that some risks are taken to keep the goals of development and discovery at the forefront. For example, committees meet with the objective of promoting an identified number of projects that will help the university meet its mandates. Emphasis is placed on not layering the decision-making process in certain areas of importance. These institutions are prime examples that protocols and policies can be developed that promote agency values. Many of these institutions have taken measures to ensure that their prime objectives will continually be met. They establish evaluation processes designed to identify institutional protocols that have been developed that might hinder the primary goals. They immediately modify and at times eliminate policies and procedures that get in the way. For other institutions of higher learning, however, the original values have been lost to the old method of eliminating behavioral variance.

Public education must avoid the pattern of attempting to eliminate all undesirable behaviors through policies and procedures. Measures must be put into place to prevent new policies and procedures from being instituted as a direct result of the bad decisions made by the minority. Schools should design their policies and procedures first and primarily to promote their main objectives. The approach is simple: seek to promote desired behaviors and practices and stop focusing on eliminating aberrations. Always ask if a new policy or procedure will help or hinder the major mandates of education. Evaluate all new policies and procedures to make sure that none of them has produced unforeseen consequences that place the focus in the wrong areas or that directly hinder the grand scheme.

CHAPTER 18

The Role of Belief in Education

Your belief determines your action and your action determines your results, but first you have to believe.

– Mark Victor Hansen

The commonly used adage "All students can learn and excel" provides an interesting paradox when viewed in light of brain science. Brain science calls into question if many educators really believe what they are saying. In the human brain, true belief is always evidenced by action.

This book has dedicated a significant number of pages to helping readers learn the role of the amygdala in human behavior. It has been established that the amygdala is the initial filter of the human brain and the holder of beliefs and values. The fact that it is the initial filter means that the screening of all stimuli is first emotional, then cognitive. Strongly held values and beliefs alter daily perceptions by helping us all focus on any stimuli encountered that support existing positions. Many studies have shown that people hear speech differently dependent on their perceptions about the person speaking. Howard Nusbaum, University of Chicago, explains that listeners' expectations are just as powerful as the actual acoustic cues. All beliefs held by the human brain work in this same manner, shaping perceptions and altering the chemical experience (Branan 2007, p. 11). Remember, microsaccades are always scanning every situation and drawing attention to anything that relates to an existing value of the amygdala. Humans are built to continuously strengthen existing positions.

The amount of passion associated with a held belief or value also can alter perceptions and prevent the rational resolution of contradictions. This means that humans have a tendency to misperceive stimuli in order to better support their existing beliefs. If someone believes that all children can learn, that person will see evidence of that position daily. However, if someone truly does not believe that all children can learn, he or she, too, will see daily evidence of that.

Since the amygdala is an action system, strongly held beliefs are usually evidenced by some level of action. The stronger the belief, the more dramatic the action and the more committed the individual becomes to maintaining the behavior. Therefore, a sincere belief that all students can learn and achieve should easily be evident to even the casual observer. All teachers consistently bear witness to their views on education. Teachers who believe all students can learn are continually dedicating themselves to maintaining effective practices and to the never-ending search for new strategies to meet the challenges of an ever-changing student population. The teacher who does not believe that all students can learn is content with the notion that since a significant number of students are learning, the failures of a few must be the fault of the students who are falling short.

The only conclusion that can be drawn when there is no evidence of the search for and commitment to practices that allow all students to maximize achievement is that there is no true belief that all pupils can learn. Belief seems to be the distinguishing feature in teachers that eventually validates the conviction that all students can learn and achieve. Belief is not just the motivator of behavior; it is also the source of unspoken communication between teacher and pupil. It is this unspoken language that resounds loudly in every student who has experienced success and encourages him to try. Remember, it is the amygdala that governs nonverbal cues exhibited by all strong emotions. Teachers who truly believe that all students can learn will loudly proclaim to every student on a daily basis, "I believe you can learn." The student will see it in the teacher's face, gestures, postures, hand movements, and hear it clearly in the tone of voice. The student will be influenced by the dedication to practices that the teacher knows to be effective. To the student who does not believe in himself or herself, it is the belief of the teacher that initially motivates the courage to attempt work and face possible failure yet again.

REFERENCES

Alessandri, SM. 1991. Play and social behavior in maltreated preschoolers. *Development and Psychopathology* 3:191–205.

Allen, RE and Oliver, JM. 1982. The effects of child maltreatment on language development. *Child Abuse and Neglect* 6(3): 299–305.

Allison, T, Puce, A, and McCarthy, G. 2000. Social perception from visual cues: role of the STS region. *Trends in Cognitive Science* 4:267–278.

Augoustinos, M. 1987. Developmental effects of child abuse: recent findings. *Child Abuse and Neglect* 11:15–27.

Azar, S.T. 1988. Methodological considerations in treatment outcome research in child maltreatment. In G. Hotaling, D. Finkelhor, J. Kirkpatrick, and M. Straus, eds. *Coping with Family Violence: Research and Policy Perspectives.* (pp. 288-298) Beverly Hills, CA: Sage Publications.

Badre, David, and Wagner, Anthony, D. 2007. Left ventrolateral prefrontal cortex and the cognitive control of memory, *Neuropsychologia* 45:2883–2901.

Battistich, V, Solomon, D, and Kim, D. 1995. Schools as communities, poverty levels of student populations, and students' attitudes, motives, and performance. *American Education Journal* 32:627–658.

Bernstein, D. A., Clarke-Stewart, A., Penner, L.A., Roy, E. J., & Wickens, C. D. 2000. *Psychology* (5th ed.) Boston: Houghton-Mifflin Company.

Birch, S. H. & Ladd, G. W. 1997. The teacher-child relationship and early school adjustment. *Journal of School Psychology* 55 (1): 61–79.

Blair, R, Monson, J, and Frederickson, N. 2001. Moral reasoning and conduct problems in children with emotional and behavioral difficulties. *Personality and Individual Difference* 31(5): 799–811.

Blair, R, Morris, J S, Firth, D, Parrett, DI, and Dolan, R J. 1999. Dissociable neural responses to facial expressions of sadness and anger. *Brain* 122(5)(May): 883–93.

Blakeslee, Sandra and Blakeslee, Matthew 2007. Where Mind and Body Meet. *Scientific American MIND* 18(2): 44–51.

Blum, Kenneth, Cull, John G, Braverman, Eric R, and Comings, David E. 1996. Reward deficit syndrome. *American Scientist* 84:132–134.

Blum, K Sheridan, P.J. Wood, R.C. Braverman, E.R. Chen, T.J.H.Cull, J.G. and Comings, D.E. 1996. The D2 dopamine receptor gene as a predictor of impulsive-addictive-compulsive behavior: Bayes' theorem. *J. Royal Society of Medicine* 89:396-400.

Branan, Nicole, 2007. See What I Say. *Scientific American MIND* 18(4) (August/September): 11.

Carlson, M, and Earls, F. 1997. Psychological and neuroendocrinological sequelae of early social deprivation in institutionalized children in Romania. *The Integrative Neurobiology of Affiliation*, New York:.New York Academy of Sciences.

Carter, CS. 1998. Neuroendocrine perspectives on social attachment and Love. *Psychoneuroendocrinology.* 23(8):779–818

Carter, CS, DeVries, AC, and Getz, LL. 1995. Physiological substrates of mammalian monogamy: the prairie vole model. *Neuroscience Biobehavior Review* 19:303–314.

Di Chiara G, Tanda, G, Bassareo, GV, Pontieri, F, Acquas, E, Fenu, S, and Carboni, E. 1999. Drug addiction as a disorder of associative learning: role of nucleus accumbens shell/extended amygdala dopamine. *Annals of the New York Academy of Sciences* 877:461–485.

Cloninger, CR. 1983. Genetic and environmental factors in the development of alcoholism. *Journal of Psychiatric Treatment Evaluation* 5:487–496.

Cooper, Jerrold S. 1973. Sumerian and Akkadian in Sumer and Akkad. *Orientalia* 42:239–246.

Damasio, Antonio, 1994. *Descartes' error: emotion, reason, and the human brain.* Penguin Books.

Davis, S F., and Palladino, JJ. 2002. *Psychology (*3rd ed). Upper Saddle River, NJ: Prentice-Hall.

Dewey, John. 1916. *Democracy and education.* New York: Macmillan.

Dias R, Robbins TW, and Roberts, AC. 1996. Dissociation in prefrontal cortex of affective and attentional shifts. *Nature* 380:69–72.

Dubin, M. 2002, *How the brain works,* Blackwell Press, Willinston, Vt.

Dodge, Kenneth A., Price, Joseph M., Bachorowski, Jo-Anne, and Newman, Joseph P. 1990. Hostile attribution bias in severely aggressive adolescents. *Journal of Abnormal Psychology* 99:385–92.

Ekman, P and Friesen, WV. 1969. The repertoire of nonverbal behavior: categories, origins, usage, and coding. *Semiotic* 1:49–98.

Elmer, E. 1977. A follow-up study of traumatized children. *Pediatrics* 59:273–279.

Egbert, R, and Kliegl, R. 2003. Microdaccades uncover the orientation of covert attention. *Vision Research* 43:1035–1045.

Fantuzzo, J W. 1990. Behavioral treatment of the victims of child abuse and neglect. *Behavior Modification* 14(3): 316–339.

Felner RD, Jackson AW, Kasak D, Mulhall P, Brand S, and Flowers, N. 1997. The impact of school reform for the middle years: longitudinal study of a network engaged in turning points-based comprehensive school transformation. *Phi Delta Kappan* 78: 528–532, 541–550.

Ferris CF. 1996. Serotonin diminishes aggression by suppressing the activity of the vasopressin system. *Ann New York Academy of Sciences* 794:98–103.

Fried, I, MacDonald, KA. and Wilson, CL. 1997. Single neuron activity in human hippocampus and amygdala during recognition of faces and objects, *Neuron* 18:753–65.

Garbarino, J. 1999. Lost boys: why our sons turn to violence and how we can save them. *Reaching Today's Youth.* 3(4): 7–10.

Garmezy, N, Masten, AS, and Tellegen, A. 1984. The study of stress and competence in children: a building block for developmental psychopathology, *Child Development* 55:97–111.

Gear, R, Aley, K, and Levine, J. 1999. Pain-induced analgesia mediated by mesolimbic reward circuits. *Journal of Neuroscience* 19(16): 7175–7181.

Givens, David B. 1986. The big and the small: toward a paleontology of gesture. *Sign Language Studies* 51(Summer): 145–167.

Givens, David B. 2005. *Isopraxism.* Center for Nonverbal Studies. http://members. aol.com/nonverbal2/tone.htm.

Goffman, Erving, 1974. *Frame analysis: An essay on the organization of experience.* Cambridge: Harvard University Press.

Goleman, D. 1995. *Emotional Intelligence.* New York: Bantam Books.

Harris, James C. 2003. Social neuroscience, empathy, brain integration, and neurodevelopmental disorders. *Psychiatry and Behavioral Sciences and Pediatrics.* 79: 525–531.

Henggler, SW., and Schoenwald, SK. 1993. Multisystemic therapy with juvenile offenders: an effective family-based treatment. *The Family Psychologist* 9:24–26.

Hoffman-Plotkin, D. and Twentyman, CT. 1984. A multimodal assessment of behavioral and cognitive deficits in abused and neglected preschoolers. *Child Development* 55:794–802.

Horvitz J. 2000. Mesolimbic and nigrostriatal dopamine responses to salient non-rewarding stimuli. *Neuroscience* 96(4): 651–656.

Iversen, SD, and Mishkin, M. 1970. Perseverative interference in monkeys following selective lesions of the inferior prefrontal convexity. *Experimental Brain Research* 11:376–86.

Johnstone, Tom and Scherer, KR. 1999. *The effects of emotions on voice quality.* In *Proceedings of the International Congress of Phonetic Sciences* (pp. 2029-2032).

Kaiser, A and Delaney, E. 1996. The effects of poverty on parenting young children. *Peabody Journal of Education* 71(4): 66–85.

Kandel, Eric, R. Schwartz, *James,* and Jessell, Thomas, 1991. *Principles of Neural Science.* New York: Elsevier.

Kiefer, Ingrid, 2007. Brain food. *Scientific American Mind* 18(5)(October/November): 58–61.

Kolko, D J. 1992. Short-term follow-up of child psychiatric hospitalization: clinical description, predictors, and correlates. *Journal of the American Academy of Child & Adolescent Psychiatry* 31:719–27.

Krugman, Martin, 1985. Neuro-linguistic programming treatment for anxiety: magic or myth? *Journal of Consulting and Clinical Psychology*. 53(4)(August): 526–530.

Lambert, Kelly. and Lilienfeld, Scott, O. 2007. Brain Stains. *Scientific American MIND* 18(5): 46–53, 106–107.

Latta, Sara, 2000. *Do you see what I'm saying? The role of gestures in learning*. http://www.brainconnection.com/topics/?main=fa/gestures.

LeDoux, J.E. 1996. *The Emotional Brain*. New York: Simon and Schuster.

Lehrer, Jonah, 2006. The reinvention of the self. *SEED* 2(3):59–67.

*Lieberman, P.*1991. Preadaptation, natural selection and function. *Language and Communication*. 11(1–2): 63–65.

Lowinson, J, Ruiz, P, Millman, R, and Langrod, J. 1997. *Substance abuse: A comprehensive Textbook* (3ʳᵈ ed) Baltimore, MD: Williams & Wilkins.

Lynch, MA., and Roberts, J. 1982. *Consequences of Child Abuse*. New York: Academic Press.

Macht, Michael. 2007. Feeding the Psyche. *Scientific American MIND* 18(5) (October/November): 65–69.

Martinez-Conde, S. 2006. Fixational eye movements in normal and pathological vision. *Progress in Brain Research* 154:151–76.

Martinez-Conde, S, Macknil, SL, Hubel, D H. 2004. The role of fixational eye movements in visual perception. *Nature Reviews Neuroscience* 5:229-240.

Martinez-Conde, S, Macknil, SL, Troncoso, X G, Dyar, TA. 2006. Microsaccades counteract visual fading during fixation. *Neuron* 49:297–305.

Martinez-Conde, S, Macknil, SL. 2007. Windows on the mind. *Scientific American MIND* 297(2): 56–63.

McAuliffe, Kathleen, 2007. Life of brain. *Discover Presents the Brain* (Spring): 6–11.

McCrone, John, 2000. *Rebels with a cause.* New Scientist Jan 22. http://www. newscientist.com/channel/being-human/teenagers/mg16522224.200.

McGrew, WC. 1972. An ethological study of children's behavior. London: Academic Press.

Mehrabian, A. 1981. *Silent messages: Implicit communication of emotions and attitudes* (2nd ed.) Belmont, California: Wadsworth.

Meltzoff, A, and Prinz, W, eds. 2002. *The imitative mind: development, evolution, and brain bases,* Cambridge: Cambridge University Press.

Motluk, A. 2001. Read My Mind. *New Scientist* 169(2275)(January 27): 22–26.

Murakami, Elaine, and Young, Jennifer, 1997. *Daily travel by persons with low income.* Paper for NPTS Symposium Bethesda, MD. Originally presented with 6-month NPTS dataset at the African American Mobility Symposium, Tampa, FL. Electronic document. http://www_cta.ornl.gov/npts/1995/Doc/LowInc.pdf.

Nelson, TE, Oxley, ZM, and Clawson, RA. 1997. Toward a psychology of framing effects. *Political Behavior* 19(3): 221–246.

Olds, D.L., Henderson, C.R. Jr., Kitzman, H., Eckenrode, J., Cole R., Tatelbaum, R. 1998. Prenatal and infancy home visitation by nurses: recent findings. *The Future of Children* 9(1): 44-65.

Offord, DR. 1992. Outcome, prognosis and risk in a longitudinal follow-up study. *Journal of American Academy of Child and Adolescent Psychiatry* 31(5): 916–923.

Pellegrino, G, Fadiga, L, Fogassi, L, Gallese, V, and Rizzolatti, G. 1992. Understanding motor events: a neurophysiological study. *Exp Brain Res* 91:176–180.

Perry, BD, Stolk, JM, and Vantini, G. 1983. Strain differences in rat brain epinephrine synthesis and alpha-adrenergic receptor number apparent 'in vivo' regulation of brain alpha – adrenergic receptors by epinephrine. *Science* 221:1297-1299.

Porter, Fran Lang, Porges, Stephen W, and Marshall, Richard E. 1988. Newborn pain cries and vagal tone: parallel changes in response to circumcision. *Child Development* 59:495–505.

Rae-Grant, N., Thomas, B.H., Offord, D.R., and Boyle, M.H. 1988. Risk, protective factors and the prevalence of behavioral and emotional disorders in children and adolescents. *Journal of American Academy of Child and Adolescent Psychiatry* 28(2): 262-268.

Ramachandran, V. S. 2000. *Mirror Neurons* www.edge.org/documents/archive/edge69.html.

Ramachandran, VS. 2004. *A brief tour of human consciousness.* New York:.PI Press.

Rizzolatt, i G, and Arbib, MA 1998. Language within our grasp. *Trends Neuroscience* 21:188–194.

Rizzolatti, Giacomo, Fogassi, Leonardo and Gallese, Vittorio 2006. Mirrors in the Mind. *Scientific American* 295(5)(November): 61.

Rolls, ET 1996. The orbitofrontal cortex. *Philosophical Transactions of the Royal Society. of London* 351:1433–1444.

Rose, Steven 2005. *The future of the brain.* Oxford, UK: Oxford University Press.

Rutter, M 1985. Resilience in the face of adversity: protective factors and resistance to psychiatric disorder. *British Journal of Psychiatry* 147:598–611.

Rutter, M 1987. Psychosocial Resilience and Protective Mechanisms. *American Journal of Orthopsychiatry* 57(3):316-31.

Salk, L. 1962. Mother's heartbeat as an imprinting stimulus. *Transact New York Academy of Sciences* 24:753-763.

Sanchez, H. 2003. *The mentor's guide to promoting resiliency.* US: Xlibris.

Scherer, KR. 1986. Vocal affect expression: a review and a model for future research. *Psychological Bulletin* 99:143–165.

Schultz, W, Tremblay, L, and Hollerman, R. 2000. Reward processing in primate orbitofrontal cortex and basal ganglia. *Cerebral Cortex* 10:272–284.

Shouse, RC, 1996. Academic press and sense of community: conflict, congruence, and implications for student achievement. *Social Psychology of Education* 1(1): 47–68.

Shure, M.B. & Spivak, G. 1988. Interpersonal cognitive problem solving. In R.H. Price, E.L. Cowen, R.P. Lorion, and J. Ramos-McKay, Eds. *Fourteen ounces of prevention: A casebook for practitioners.* (pp. 69-82). Washington, DC: American Psychological Association. Solomon, D, Battistich, V, Watson M, Schapsci E, and Lewis, C. 2000. A six-district study of educational change: direct and mediated effects of the child development project. *Social Psychology of Education* 4:3–51.

Sylwester, R. 2002. *Mirror Neurons.* Brain Connection. *http://www.brainconnection. com/content/181_1.*

Tierney, JP. 1995. Making a difference: an impact study of big brothers/big sisters. *Public/Private Ventures.* Philadelphia, PA. Quoted in: National Campaign to Prevent Teen Pregnancy. 1998. Start Early, Stay Late. op. cit.

Uvnas-Moberg, K 1997. Physiological and endocrine effects of social contact. *Ann New York Academy of Science* 807:146-163.

Uvnas-Moberg K. 1998. Oxytocin May Mediate the Benefits of Positive Social Interaction and Emotions. *Psychoneuroendocrinology* 23(8)(Nov): 819–835.

Uvnas-Moberg K. 2003. Oxytocin may mediate the benefits of positive social interaction and emotions. *Psychoneuroendocrinology* **23(1998):** 819–835.

Uvnas-Moberg, Kerstin. 2003. *The oxytocin factor: tapping the hormone of calm, love, and healing.* Cambridge, MA: Da Capo Press.

Vance, *J. Eric M.D., Bowen, Natasha K. PH.D., Fernandez, Gustavo PH.D., Thompson, Shealy PH.D. 2002.* Risk and protective factors as predictors of outcome in adolescents with psychiatric disorder and aggression. *Journal of the American Academy of Child & Adolescent Psychiatry* 41(1)(January): 36–43.

Vance, J.E., and Sanchez, H. 1994. *Delivering resiliency to those at risk.* http://www.dhhs. state.nc.us/mhddsas/childandfamily/technicalassistance/risk_and_resiliency.htm.

Volkow, N.D., and Fowler, J.S. 2000. Addiction, a disease of compulsion and drive: involvement of the orbitofrontal cortex. *Cerebral Cortex* 10:318–325.

Wachsmuth, Ipke. 2006. Gestures offer insight. *Scientific American MIND* (October) http://www.sciammind.com/article.cfm?articleID=000EABAF-AE71-1522-A5A283414B7F0000&ref=sciam.

Wenner, Melinda 2007. Everyone Agrees. *Scientific American MIND* 18(4) (August/ September): 13.

Werner, EE. 1989. High risk children in young adulthood: a longitudinal study from birth to 32 years. *American Journal of Orthopsychiatry* 59(1): 72–81.

Werner, EE. 2000. Protective factors and individual resilience In Meisels, SJ and Shonkof, JP, eds. *Handbook of Early Childhood Intervention.* (2nd) (pp. 97–116) New York: Cambridge University Press.

Werner, EE. 2000. Protective factors and individual resilience. In Shonkoff, JP and Meisles, S. editor. *Handbook of Early Childhood Intervention.* (2nd) New York: Cambridge University Press.

Werner, EE., and Smith, RS 1982. *Vulnerable but invincible: a longitudinal study of resilient children and youth.* New York: McGraw-Hill.

Werner, EE. and Smith RS. 1992. *Overcoming the odds: high risk children from birth to adulthood.* Ithaca, NY: Cornell University Press.

Wyman, PA. 1991. Interviews with children who experienced major life stress: family and child attributes that predict resilient outcomes. *Journal of American Academy of Child and Adolescent Psychiatry* 31(5): 904–910.

Zimrin, H. 1986. A profile of survival. *Child Abuse and Neglect* 10:339–349.

Zins, J E, and Ponti, C. 1990. Best practices in school-based consultation. In A. Thomas and Grimes J, Eds. *Best Practices in School Psychology II (*pp. 673–94) Washington, DC: National Association of School Psychologists.

Zubieta, JK, Heitzeg, MM, Smith, YR, Bueller, JA, Xu, K, Xu, Y, Koeppe, RA, Stohler, CS, and Goldman, D. 2003. COMT val158met genotype affects muopioid neurotransmitter responses to a pain stressor. *Science* 299:1240–1243.

INDEX